A story, a hug and a prayer 3

A story, a hug and a prayer 3

A family bedtime book by Michael Forster

First published in 2004 by
KEVIN MAYHEW LTD
Buxhall, Stowmarket, Suffolk, IP14 3BW
E-mail: info@kevinmayhewltd.com

KINGSGATE PUBLISHING INC
1000 Pannell Street, Suite G, Columbia, MO 65201
E-mail: sales@kingsgatepublishing.com

© 2004 Michael Forster

The right of Michael Forster to be identified as the author
of this work has been asserted by him in accordance with
the Copyright, Designs and Patents Act 1988.

All rights reserved. No part of this publication may be
reproduced, stored in a retrieval system, or transmitted,
in any form or by any means, electronic, mechanical,
photocopying, recording or otherwise, without the
prior written permission of the publisher.

9 8 7 6 5 4 3 2 1 0

ISBN 1 84417 184 1
Catalogue No. 1500669

Cover illustration by Steve English
Cover design by Trace Price
Edited by Graham Harris
Typesetting by Louise Selfe

Printed and bound in Great Britain

Contents

Foreword	7
I am my brother's *brother*!	9
The little world of Captain Noah	13
The power tower	17
Cunning plans	21
God sets his people free	25
Rules for free people	29
All that glisters is not God	33
Mixed marriage, mixed monarchy	37
Brains before brawn	41
Prophet and loss	45
Elijah listens and learns	49
I may be little, but I matter	53
This isn't happening!	57
Healing Naaman's prejudices	61
God has hidden depths	65
Peter goes over the top	69
Forgiven and unforgiving	73
You mean you didn't even try?	77
Jesus on the edge	81
Faith raises the roof	85
Moses, Elijah and Jesus	89
It's a power thing	93
The boy Jesus in the temple	97
Jesus challenges us with love	101
Lots of love	105
Love is a seed to be sown	109
Taking the time to care	113
God's basic law of love	117

For love or money	121
Gee Whiz	125
Don't miss the party	129
Seth in a sweat	133
Healing of 10 lepers	137
Danny sees the light	141
He's the greatest!	145
He's alive!	149
Chateau heaven, '27	153
Help me feed the world	157
Sore feet and toffee noses	161
Forgiveness that hurts	165

Foreword

You know, I sometimes feel a little sorry for God. Most of us seem to think that when we spend time with him we have to talk at him. Now, I'm sure God likes a good conversation as much as anyone does, but isn't there more to life than that? Might he also like just to be with us, to play with us, to hang out with us?

This series of books began with a cry for help. 'I can't pray with my children: can you write something?' We decided to get away from the old 'Hands together, eyes closed' formula (which had never worked for me in 50 years) and invite God to share in telling the children a bedtime story – with plenty of hugs along the way – and enjoy being part of the ordinary family relationships.

Some people have been kind enough to say that these books have changed the way they pray with their children. I'm delighted – because in that case the way they relate to God – which is what prayer really is – must surely have changed, too.

While using this book, you might break off the prayer to let the children add something – or even have a conversation about what's being prayed for. It'll still be prayer because God won't stop listening – in fact he might use the conversation to help you hear what he's saying to you!

Enjoy the book.
Enjoy each other.
And enjoy God!

Michael Forster

I am my brother's **brother!**

Based on Genesis 4:1-16

Adam and Eve (remember them – the first people God made?) – well, they had a couple of sons called Cain and Abel. Now, of course, all brothers and sisters quarrel occasionally, but with Cain and Abel it was a way of life. Whatever one of them said, the other would disagree just for the sake of it and before the next sparrow chirped there'd be tears and tantrums.

'I worry about those two,' said Eve. 'One day, one of them's going to draw blood.'

'Oh, I don't think so,' Adam answered. 'They've never been any good at art. But I'm seriously afraid one of them might get hurt if they don't stop quarrelling.'

Before Eve could reply, there were raised voices on the terrace. 'You give me that back – it's mine.'

'You haven't played with it for ages.'

'Well, I want to now.'

'Well you can't, so there.'

Now, if you're hoping they'd grow out of this silliness, you've got another think coming. The words changed as they grew older, but it was essentially the same argument.

'You've ruined my cabbage crop!' Cain roared at Abel. 'You and those lousy sheep of yours.'

'Well, where are they supposed to graze?' bellowed Abel. 'You've planted crops on every inch of land, you greedy parasite and there's nothing left for me to use.'

'Don't call me a parasite.'

'I'll call you whatever I want.'

'No you won't.'

'Yes, I will.'

A story, a hug and a prayer

And so it went on, until they'd completely forgotten what the real argument was about.

The day came when Abel – who, as you may have gathered, was a shepherd – decided to give God a present. 'The very best lamb I've got,' he said. 'Only that will be good enough for God.'

When Cain heard about it, he was hopping mad. 'Trying to get God on his side, is he?' he seethed. 'I'll show him what crawling's really about.' He gathered the best fruit and vegetables from his crops* – and took them to where Abel was praying. 'There you are, God!' he crowed. 'Better than a pathetic little lamb, eh? Just so that you know, I'm your man – I'm the one to back around this joint. OK?'

God wasn't pleased. 'Is this what you think it's all about?' he demanded. 'Trying to get me on your side? Well, I'm happy with Abel's gift, thank you very much – *he's* being honest. And don't glower at me like that, either – I don't frighten that easily. Look, Cain, I'd get a grip on that temper if I were you, while you still can.'

'Yeah, yeah, I know,' sneered Cain and stormed off. Later, he said to Abel, 'Fancy a walk in the fields?'

Abel should have known better, but he didn't. He went off with Cain, and guess what – next thing he knew, he was dead. Cain's temper had finally got the better of him. As he was walking home, wondering what to say to Adam and Eve, Cain heard God's voice.

'Hi, Cain – where's Abel?'

'What am I,' Cain sulked, 'My brother's keeper?'

'I know what you've done,' God said. 'I can hear his very blood crying out from the ground for justice – the same ground you expect to give you crops to eat, now fouled with your own brother's blood. Well, that's the end of all that. You're a man on the run, now.'

'I can't run anywhere,' Cain objected. 'Anyone who finds me will kill me.'

God sounded really stern, now. 'You don't get off that

---

* Like what, for instance? Can we think of some examples?

I am my brother's brother!

lightly,' he said. 'I'll make sure you have to live with this for a long time. Now, go.'

So Cain ended up in the land of Nod. Oh, don't get me wrong – sleep wasn't part of the deal, not with Cain's conscience. Nod was the name of another country.

That's where Cain went, and that's where our story ends. Because no one has every heard any more of either Cain or Nod since that time.

A story, a hug and a prayer

Let's chat . . .

> It's all too easy to 'win' a fight or an argument
> only to find we've lost what's really important to us.
> I often think that when Cain was on the run
> he must often have wished he'd never started that fight!

We're sad . . .

> Lord Jesus,
> we're sorry for the times we hurt each other
> because we're jealous or angry.
> We know it hurts you, too.
> Please forgive us.

We're glad . . .

> Thank you, Jesus, for loving us
> and for wanting us to have a really good life.
> Thank you for all the things you give us,
> especially each other.

Let's pray for people . . .

> Please, God, bless all families,
> especially the unhappy ones
> where people damage one another.
> Please bless us, too,
> and help us to be truly loving.

The little world of Captain Noah

Based on Genesis 7:11-24

Can you imagine being cooped up on a boat for three months with your family? Oh, and a few animals as well – like two of every kind in the whole world? That, by the way, includes two snakes, two big, hairy spiders, two cockroaches, and a pair of fleas in a jam jar with a loose lid.

It all began months earlier when God decided to start again. The world had gone really mad – people were being cruel to each other, fighting over all the wonderful things God had put in creation; everyone cared more about getting rich than getting friends. It really was grim – but there was just one really good family.

Any idea who they were? Yes, Noah – along with his wife, his children and his grandchildren. They were good people – cared for each other, knew what really mattered in life, and all that stuff. So, God decided he wanted to use them as the basis of a whole new world.

That's how Noah ended up in the shipbuilding industry. 'I'm going to make it rain like it's never rained before,' God told him. 'So you've got to build the biggest lifeboat in history and get two of every kind of animal on board before everything's flooded.'

Which is how we come to find Noah, in his ark, scratching his head, wondering why it's itching, and holding in his hand the jam jar that used to have the fleas in it. 'I don't want to be ungrateful, God,' he says. 'I mean, it's good of you to save us all from the flood, but wasn't there any other way?'

'Think of it as a chance to practise social skills, Noah,' God answers, 'If you lot can get along together on the ark,

A story, a hug and a prayer

you shouldn't have too much trouble when you're back in the great, wide world.'

So there they are – Noah, his wife, their three sons, who are called Shem, Ham and Japheth, and *their* wives – and two of every kind of creature in the world.*

They're stuck there on that ark for five months. For the first 40 days it rains – continuously – so they can't even go for a walk on deck.

You can just hear the children complaining:

'I want to go out.'

'There's nothing to do in this place.'

Actually, there's plenty to do – just not the things they like.

'If you're bored, try mucking out the elephants,' Noah tells them. 'That should keep you quiet for a few days.'

Then Shem interrupts: 'And whose turn was it to feed the tigers last night – because whoever it was, they didn't. The last thing I need is to be stuck on a boat with hungry tigers.'

'I can cope with hungry tigers,' Mrs Noah answers. 'It's all your snoring that bothers me.'

'I'm fed up with this boat,' moans one of the grandchildren. 'I want to get off.'

'Get off?' Noah answers. 'Get off? Where d'you think you're going to go?'

And all this time, the water's getting deeper and deeper, and even the mountaintops have disappeared. So there really isn't anywhere.

By the time the five months are up, you can imagine what life in the ark's like. Then the water starts to go down, and land appears – and soon they can leave their floating home for dry land.

'Great,' we can hear Shem saying. 'We've got all this world to ourselves – we'll never be overcrowded again, so we can all just do as we like.'

But God's got other ideas. 'Not that simple,' he says. 'I

---

* Here you could have fun seeing how many different animals you can name together.

The little world of Captain Noah

want lots more – animals and people. You've got to fill the earth with life again.'

'Oh, great!' says Shem. 'So it's still going to be crowded.

'And we're still going to be stuck with each other,' Ham adds.

'Got it in one,' says God. 'So I hope you've all learned something about getting along together.'

A story, a hug and a prayer

Let's chat . . .

> I suppose the world's a bit like the ark, isn't it?
> We're all stuck on it together,
> and it's getting more crowded all the time,
> and we've really got to learn to get along.

We're sad . . .

> We're sorry, God,
> for the way we sometimes make life difficult
> for ourselves as well as for others.
> Please help all your people to share our space
> so that we can have peace in our world.

We're glad . . .

> Actually, God, we know we often complain a lot,
> but really we're glad to be a bit crowded.
> We like being close to people, and to animals,
> and we want to thank you for all the beauty
> you've put into your world – our 'ark'.

Let's pray for people . . .

> Some people live in really crowded places,
> and there's not much fun in that.
> Please, God, help the people in your world
> to share the space you've given us
> so that everyone can have enough.

The power tower

Based on Genesis 11:1-9

Let me tell you about Barney. Now, Barney was really a nice guy, but his trouble was that he just got carried away by wild schemes and didn't always remember what *really* mattered. Now, at this time, the people in the world were all speaking the same language and getting along together pretty well – that was until Barney had one of his *big ideas*.

It all began one starry night: he was standing staring into the sky when his friend Zack came along. 'Hi, Barney, what's up?'

Barney pointed excitedly to the sky. 'You tell me, Zack,' he urged him. 'Look up and tell me what you see.'

Zack looked up. 'Sky,' he said. 'Nice lighting.'

'Barney, you've got no vision!' Zack said. 'Let me tell you what I see. I see *power*.'

'Oh,' said Zack, sounding breathtakingly unimpressed. 'Power.'

'And *fame!*' added Barney.

'Ah, yes,' Zack mused, quietly. 'Power and fame. Well, as long as they both stay up there, out of my way . . .'

Barney wasn't put off, though. His big idea was getting bigger all the time, and soon he was spreading it all around the neighbourhood. 'Let's build a tower!' he urged everybody. 'Then we'll have power, and we'll have fame, and no one will be able to push us around and we'll be able to do exactly what we like.'

Zack tried to reason with him. 'What if other people build towers, too?' he asked. 'And what if their towers are bigger than yours?'

'They won't be!' Barney answered. 'And if they are, I'll just go and knock them down.'

A story, a hug and a prayer

'Oh, of course!' Barney answered. 'So it's a power game.'

'Game?' Barney was horrified. 'It's no game. I'm deadly serious.'

Barney soon convinced most of the people to back his idea, and I've got to admit that the tower soon started looking really impressive. The only person other than Zack who didn't seem happy about it was Barney's girlfriend, Prudence. 'I just know he'll get completely carried away,' she told Zack, 'and he'll forget what's important in his life.' Well, she had to talk to Zack, because Barney wasn't listening to her – in fact he seemed to have forgotten she existed. All his time was taken up with planning meetings, site surveys, and checking that none of the other communities around them was building a bigger tower. Whenever the workers got greedy and asked for more money he'd say: 'Money isn't everything – think of the fame. Trust me. Everybody will be famous!' It never seemed to occur to him that if everybody's famous, then famous is ordinary – which means that nobody's famous! That, however, is a profound thought, and there's no room for those in a head that's already full of big ideas.

One night, when it was quiet, God came and had a look around. 'I've got to stop this,' he said. 'There'll be no holding this lot if it gets any further off the ground. Why, the whole of my beautiful creation could be ruined by big ideas like this. But not to worry . . . I have a cunning plan . . .'

So, next morning, when Barney went to the building site, he had a shock in store. No one was doing any work at all. They were all standing in little groups, shouting at each other and waving their arms about. Barney went up to his site manager and said, 'What's going on – why aren't the men working?'

Peter, the site manager – who for some reason seemed to have changed his name to Pierre – stared at him and said, '*Pardon monsieur?*'

Barney turned to the foreman. 'What's he on about, Charlie?'

Carlos shrugged his shoulders. '*No comprendez, senor!*'

The power tower

Have you got it? D'you see God's cunning plan? Suddenly, they were all speaking different languages, and no one could understand a word anybody else was saying. (Mind you, you don't need to speak different languages for that to happen, but that's another story . . .) So, the work on the tower stopped, and the workers all went to live in different places. Barney's dreams were in tatters, and he was a very sad man. 'I've lost everything,' he said. 'All that power, all that fame – it's all gone and I've got nothing at all.'

'Yes you have,' said a gentle voice. 'We're still around.'

Barney turned and saw Zack and Prudence. 'Oh, yes,' he said, with a relieved smile. 'I'd forgotten about you.'

I think he'd forgotten about a lot of things – don't you?

A story, a hug and a prayer

Let's chat . . .

*There's nothing necessarily wrong with power and fame,
as long as we control them
– and they don't control us!
That's easier said than done, though.
But I think Barney's just realised
that real happiness lies elsewhere.
Can you see what I mean?*

We're sad . . .

*Loving God,
please forgive us when we lose sight
of what really matters.
We're sorry for the way we sometimes go
chasing after things that aren't worth it
when we could put all that energy
into our friendships.*

We're glad . . .

*Thank you, Jesus,
for friends, for family, for freedom,
for blue skies and glistening raindrops.
Thank you for all the important things in life.*

Let's pray for people . . .

*We pray for people who are powerful,
and for those who are famous,
especially those who are finding
it's not all the way they expected.
Please help people under pressure
to remember the ones who love them
and the things that really matter.*

Cunning plans

Based on Exodus 1:22-2:10

Imagine that you've got a new baby in the family – and he's in great danger. You've got to hide him before the wicked king can get to him. Any ideas?*

Well, let me take you to a land far away, and a time long ago. The evil king, Pharaoh, is hatching a horrible plan. 'These Israelites,' he says, 'I hate them. Why couldn't they have stayed in their own country? They're going to take over all of Egypt, that's what. Well, I'm going to stop them.'

Of course, everybody listens – they all want to know what cunning plan Pharaoh has for getting rid of all the foreign people in Egypt. 'Kill all the boy babies,' he says. 'Then they won't grow into men and attack me, will they? Then I can do exactly what I want.'

Meanwhile, in a little shack, an Israelite mother has just had a baby – and it's a boy. 'What are we going to do?' she says. 'If the king finds out he'll have him killed!'

Well, the first three months are OK – they just keep him well hidden and nobody knows he's there. But it can't go on, can it?

'It's no good,' Mum says. 'We're going to have to find somewhere else to hide him.' And that's when she gets the most amazing idea.

''We'll make him a basket out of reeds,' she says, 'and we'll seal it with tar so it'll float – and we can hide it among the rushes at the side of the river.'

Her daughter, Miriam, thinks she's really lost it! 'Mother, you're mad!' she tells her. 'What if something horrible happens to him? What if he drowns?'

---

* Pause to think of suggestions

A story, a hug and a prayer

'Ah, but he won't,' Mother answers. 'Because you'll be watching – won't you!'

So, that's how Miriam ends up hiding in the bushes near the River Nile, watching a basket hidden in the rushes. Then something terrible happens: somebody comes for a swim. And that somebody isn't just anybody, it's a royal body! This is the daughter of the king – the same one who's frightened of foreigners and wants to kill all their babies! She goes into the river, and of course, she sees the basket. 'Hey, you – servant-person!' she calls. 'Get me that basket, so I can see what's in it.'

Miriam's shaking like a leaf, in the bushes, thinking that her little brother's for the chop at any moment. The princess opens the basket, and looks in.

'It's a baby boy!' she says. 'Hey, I bet it's one of those Israelite babies. I reckon the mother's hidden it to try and fool my dad.'

Miriam's really worried, now, of course – but she can't do anything. Suddenly, the princess smiles!

'Well, yippy skip for her!' she says. 'It's about time one of them put one over on old Dad – he's been getting worse, you know, but don't tell him I said that. Tell you what, let's take the baby home.'

Naturally, the maid's a bit alarmed at this. 'Take him home?' she echoes. 'Have you gone mad – er, Your Royal Highness? What'll the king do?'

'Oh, he'll never notice,' the princess says. 'One more child in the palace will be neither here nor there. Let's go.'

Well, Miriam's got to think fast, hasn't she! Before she's had time to work out all the details, she's on her feet, calling to the princess.

'Um, excuse me, Your, er, Gloriousness – I couldn't help overhearing, just now – just sitting in the bushes counting butterflies, the way you do – but I know a slave who'd make a really good nanny.'

Naturally, the princess is a bit taken aback at first – not every day she gets shouted at from the bushes while she's having a swim and kidnapping a baby. 'Oh, OK, then – sounds a good idea,' she answers.

Cunning plans

So there's Miriam, running like she's never run before, to get her mum.

'Hey, Mum – they've found him – but it's OK – he's going to be a prince – and they want you to be his nanny.'

Meanwhile, the princess is thinking, 'What are we going to call him? He's got to have a name of some sort. I know – I'll call him Moses, because I took him out of the water.'

So it all ends up with Moses being taken to the royal household, right under Pharaoh's nose, and completely behind his back – if you see what I mean – to be brought up by his own mother who everyone thinks is his nanny.

And that's just the beginning, folks.

A story, a hug and a prayer

Let's chat . . .

> *Poor old Pharaoh – he thinks everyone's out to get him!*
> *Mind you, the way he's going on, they soon will!*
> *People like him usually turn out to be right,*
> *because they make everybody hate them!*

We're sad . . .

> *We're sorry, God, for the times we ill-treat others*
> *because of our own fears.*
> *Help us to get rid of our enemies*
> *by turning them into friends!*

We're glad . . .

> *Thank you, Jesus, for good politicians,*
> *fair judges, honest police officers.*
> *We know that sometimes bad people get power,*
> *but thank you for all the good ones*
> *who use it well.*

Let's pray for people . . .

> *We pray for people who are suffering*
> *because powerful people are afraid of them.*
> *We pray for victims of injustice, wherever they are.*
> *Loving God, challenge all leaders with your love.*

God sets his people free

Based roughly on Exodus 7:14-12:51

Today, we're in ancient Egypt again. Moses has grown up, and God's chosen him for a very special job. 'You're going to set my people free,' he's told Moses. 'The Israelites are not going to be slaves any more, because I'm going to lead them to a land of their own. Now, you go and tell Pharaoh that.'

Now, Pharaoh, the wicked king of Egypt, isn't the kind of person you tell what to do – but Moses can probably get away with it, because he knows him. All the same, though, he really has to twist Pharaoh's arm. 'If you don't stop ill-treating God's people,' he says, 'God's going to make your life really horrible.'

Well, of course, Pharaoh doesn't believe in the God of Moses, so he just laughs at him – until the plagues start. God and Moses try everything. God shows his power by turning the river water to blood, but Pharaoh won't give in. God fills the country with frogs, and then there are gnats, and flies – getting into everything, crawling all over people's dinner, hiding in their clothes – but Pharaoh still says no. Then the animals all die, and the people get boils, but Pharaoh refuses to take notice. Then the big storms start – hail and lightning like you've never seen – and after that comes the Great Darkness – darkness so thick you can feel it. And still Pharaoh won't budge. 'Get out of my sight!' he yells at Moses. 'If ever I see you again, you're dead. Got it?'

So God speaks to Moses again. 'Right,' he says, 'I hoped I wouldn't have to do this, but we're really going to have to hit Pharaoh hard to make him let my people go. Tell the Israelites to hold special dinners in their homes. They're to

A story, a hug and a prayer

eat lamb, and before they cook it they've got to put some of its blood on the doorposts of their homes. Because at midnight, I'm going to bring death to every Egyptian household – but the houses with the lambs' blood on them will be safely passed over. Now, make sure they all do it – OK?'

Well, what can Moses say? 'OK, God – you're the boss.'

But God isn't finished, yet. 'Now,' he says, 'the bread for the meal – don't use any yeast in it because you haven't got time for all that palaver. Things are really happening fast, now. You're all to be dressed ready for a journey – shoes, outdoor clothes, walking sticks, the lot – because I'm not going to be hanging around. And from now on, you'll celebrate this day every year as a festival, because this is the night I'm setting you free.'

Well, the people are amazed. 'Bread without yeast?' the women say. 'We're proud of our bread, we are – what's it going to be like if we don't do it properly?'

But Moses insists. 'No yeast, no time!' he says. 'Hats and coats on, shoes on your feet, and whatever you do, don't forget the blood on the doorposts.'

So there they are – around the dinner tables in their homes, with the blood painted on the doorposts, eating their roast lamb and this strange bread made without yeast – and the angel of death passes over the houses, looking for the Egyptian homes. Suddenly, there's terrible wailing and crying. Every Egyptian house has someone who's been killed – and in the cowsheds and chicken pens as well, some of the animals die. Even the eldest son of Pharaoh doesn't escape.

Well, that does it! Pharaoh calls for Moses and his brother Aaron. 'Get out of my country!' he bellows at them. 'I don't want anything more to do with you, or your people, or your terrible God!'

So the Israelites don't waste any time. They've already got their coats and hats on; they've got shoes on their feet and walking sticks in their hands, and they've got a supply of dough to make that funny instant bread – so they won't starve in the desert. They're up and off, with their

God sets his people free

children, their animals and whatever they can carry on the journey.

Through the streets they walk, toward the border of Egypt, and all the way, Egyptians are coming out of their houses and urging them on. They're not just *letting* their slaves go – they're positively begging them to! The Israelites reach the border, and walk across it. They're free! No more slaving in the hot sun while the Egyptians have a siesta – no more being beaten for not working hard enough – no more chains, and whips, and insults about being Israelites. They're free – free to be God's own people!

They look around, and where do you think God's taken them? The Promised Land? Or maybe a beautiful garden? Or possibly a holiday camp with lots to eat and to do? No: they're in a desert. Nothing but sand for miles and miles. 'How are we going to find our way across that?' they say. 'Where's this land of our own that God promised us? What about all the milk and honey we were expecting to find?'

'Oh, don't worry, God's going to get us there,' Moses tells them. 'This isn't the end of the story – it's just the beginning of the most exciting journey of all time!'

A story, a hug and a prayer

Let's chat . . .

*Have you ever missed an opportunity
because you weren't ready?
That's why the Israelites were told to eat
with their walking clothes on
and their bags packed.*

We're sad . . .

*Loving God,
we don't always listen to you very well.
We miss the chances you give us
to help others, or to make new friends,
or perhaps just to enjoy life more.
Please forgive us and teach us to listen
– to you and to each other!*

We're glad . . .

*We really want to thank you, God,
for being there for us.
Thank you for always wanting the best for us
and leading us toward new life.*

Let's pray for people . . .

*Some people seem to have fewer opportunities
because they're trapped in some way.
Lord Jesus, we pray for all people who are slaves,
whether to other people or to addictions of various kinds.*
Please give them new opportunities,
and help them to take them.*

---

* Mine's chocolate – what's yours! (That's why I try not to judge people who are addicted to other things!)

Rules for free people

Based on Exodus 18:13-20:17

The Israelites have left Egypt, so they're not slaves any more, and they're on their way to the land God's promised them. Moses is the one God's chosen to lead them – and what d'you think he's spending all his time doing? Settling arguments – that's what. They just can't stop wrangling among themselves, and then Moses has to sort it out. His father-in-law, Jethro, notices. 'Hey, what's going on?' he says. 'Why are you spending your time settling quarrels – with long queues of people waiting around all day to see you when they should have work to do?'

'Someone's got to do it,' Moses says. 'When they have a quarrel, I tell them who's right.'

Jethro thinks Moses is doing it the hard way, and tells him so. 'You need help,' he says. 'Why not appoint judges to do this for you? You can tell everyone what God's rules are, and then the judges will be able to decide who's right and who's wrong. Of course, they can still bring the really difficult arguments to you, but you won't be worn out, and they'll get their problems sorted.'

Well, that sounds good to Moses, so he does it – appoints good people as judges to settle arguments. But, hang on a minute – if you've got judges, you need laws, don't you?

Now, as it happens, the Israelites are camped near a big mountain, called Mount Sinai – so Moses hoofs it up the mountain to get a bit of peace and quiet and listen to God.

It's really strange up there, with thick clouds and smoke – because God's chosen to show himself to Moses

A story, a hug and a prayer

in fire.* So it's dark, hot, and no place to be if you've got asthma.

'This is our place,' God says to Moses. 'Yours and mine. The rest of the people can wait expectantly at the bottom of the hill. *Are* the people waiting expectantly?'

'Oh, yes, Lord,' Moses assures him. 'They're all waiting. Expectantly.'

'Then you'd better go back down and make sure they don't get any big ideas and start to follow you,' God tells him. 'And while you're down there, you can fetch your brother Aaron and bring him up here to me.'

So, Moses has to go all the way back down, give them the message, and then bring Aaron back up the mountain. Then God lays down the law. 'I'm God,' he says, 'and don't you forget it. Remember *I* set you free, and don't go worshipping other gods, because it won't do you any good. OK?'

'OK, God, you're the boss,' Moses and Aaron say.

'Good,' says God. 'And I don't want you making statues to worship, either. Oh, yes, I know it goes on, but I'm too great to be represented by a statue – or a picture, come to that – so it's me you're going to worship.

'And another thing. Don't use my name in bad ways.'

Moses and Aaron aren't too sure what that means. 'You mean, like using it as a swear word?'

'Yes, and other things, too,' God tells them.† 'Anyway, moving on: have a special day for rest and worship – a holy day when you can listen to me, and think about things that are really important – and yes, I know you do that every day, but once a week you can make a point of it. Got it?'

'Oh, yes, God,' Moses and Aaron say, 'We've got it.'

'Good,' God says. 'Now, that's about you and me. I've got some more rules, and they're about you and each

---

* Can the children think of another time when God showed himself to Moses in fire?

† Like what? Any ideas? (What about being dishonest when we know people will trust us because we're Christians – would that be one? Or, perhaps, saying 'God has told me this,' just to get our own way?)

Rules for free people

other. And it all starts with respect – respect your parents, because that's your first step to long life and happiness in the new land I'm giving you. And respect for others is what it's all about, really – like, if you respect people, you won't kill them, will you? Husbands and wives won't cheat on one another, and you won't take things that don't belong to you – no, not even to borrow, unless you ask first.'

Aaron looks a bit embarrassed at this. 'You know that hammer you lost, Moses? Well, I'll give it back to you when we get home.'

'Moving quickly on,' God continues, 'don't tell lies about people. And don't come that "sticks and stones" rubbish with me, either. Words *do* hurt – and gossip ruins lives. So don't do it. OK?'

'OK, God – you're the boss.'

'Finally,' says God, 'if you want to be really safe, "Don't do it" isn't enough. It's "Don't even think about it." Don't even think about wanting what other people have got – whether it's gismos, gadgets, goats or girlfriends. And the same goes for boyfriends, too. No special privileges for the girls! Now, tell the people to keep those 10 rules and they won't go far wrong.'

'Oh, yes,' says Aaron. 'We'll all keep them all the time.'

Well, if they had they might have got on a little better. But we all know how hard keeping the rules can be, don't we?

A story, a hug and a prayer

Let's chat . . .

We need some 'rules', don't we?
That doesn't mean we always like or respect them,
though.
What rules do you find the hardest to keep (or to respect)?
Can you think why they've been put there?

We're sad . . .

Forgive us, Jesus,
when we only see the rules and not the love behind them.
Help us to remember that they're made for people
– and it's the people that matter!

We're glad . . .

Thank you, God, for an ordered world.
Thank you for 'scientific laws' – like gravity
that stops us floating off into space!
Thank you for everything that helps us to be safe
and truly to live.

Let's pray for people . . .

We pray for people who suffer
because of lawlessness,
where evil appears to rule
and the only law seems to be survival.
Please, God, help people who try to transform such places
with your law of love.

All that glisters is not God

Based on Exodus 32:1-24

Aaron – Moses' brother – was having a bit of bother. Nothing unusual in that – ever since God had set the Israelites free from slavery, they seemed to have done nothing but moan. 'Where's Moses?' they were demanding.

'Up the mountain, talking to God,' was the answer, but it wasn't good enough for them.

'He's been ages!' said Danny – a known troublemaker. 'For all we know, he's died up there – then what'll we do? You'll have to make us a god to lead us the rest of the way.'

Now, with all the crowd roaring its agreement, and fists being waved in the air, this was so not the time to point out that they already had a God – the one Moses was in conference with – who'd done a pretty spectacular job so far.

Aaron decided he couldn't beat them, so he'd better please them. 'OK, OK – give me your gold earrings and I'll see what I can do.'

Meanwhile, up the mountain, God had just finished giving Moses the first laws – the Ten Commandments. 'I think you'd better be getting back, Moses,' God said. 'They've made a toy god to worship – a golden calf, of all things! And they're giving it all the credit for setting them free. Now, that would make my blood boil if I had any. You'd better get out of here before I explode – I've got no quarrel with you personally, but I've had it with them and they're going to learn that if it's the last thing they ever do learn. In fact it will be – from now on it'll be just you and me.'

Moses didn't like the sound of that. 'Oh, please, God – don't throw it all away, now. I mean, why give the Egyptians

A story, a hug and a prayer

the satisfaction? They'll laugh at you because you set your people free only to kill them yourself – and after all you promised Abraham and his family, too. Look, give me a chance to sort it, OK?'

Moses picked up the stones he'd used to write the laws on and started back down the mountain. His friend Joshua was with him, and as they got near the camp Joshua said, 'Can you hear that noise? Sounds like a battle going on.'

'That's no battle,' Moses said. 'They're celebrating.'

As they got closer, Moses could hardly believe what he was seeing. Just as God had said, they'd got the calf on a pedestal and were dancing around, singing praises to it. Moses totally lost his rag and threw the stones with the new laws on them down to the ground so that they smashed to pieces. Then he stormed over to the altar, grabbed the golden calf and threw it into the fire, before grinding the whole thing down into dust.

'Hey!' Danny shouted. My best earrings are in that statue!'

'Don't worry,' Moses grunted. 'You'll get your share of it.' Then he mixed the gold dust with water and – you'll never guess – he made the people drink it. Well, they soon found that it wasn't a god, then. God lives in people, and he'd never made their tummies rumble the way that gold dust did!

'Let that be a lesson to you,' Moses said. Then he turned to Aaron. 'What have these people ever done to you?' he demanded. 'What've they done to deserve what you've put them through? Well?'

'Don't blame me,' Aaron whined. 'You know these people – obsessed with all the wrong things. It was all their fault – they made me do it. All I did was collect up the gold, put it in the fire and out came this calf – just like that!'

Now, you know and I know that it didn't happen 'just like that' – Aaron had a lot more to with it than he wanted to admit, and trying to blame other people just made him look like a total loser! Still, he obviously learnt his lesson because he became a great servant of God – eventually!

All that glisters is not God

Let's chat . . .

*Now, there's nothing actually wrong with either gold or
calves, is there?
Until, that is, we treat them like gods!
Nothing wrong with computers, or video games, either,
or cars, or houses, or . . . well, you get my point.
They're all wonderful tools in our lives.
It's just that they're terrible gods!*

We're sad . . .

*Sometimes, God, we get things out of proportion.
The things you give us to use
start taking over our lives.
Please forgive us when we lose sight of you
and the kind of life you could give us.*

We're glad . . .

*Thank you, God, for life!
And thank you for all the things that make it really good,
whether they're hi-tech, low-tech
or just not tech at all!
Thank you for all the good things we enjoy!*

Let's pray for people . . .

We pray for people who have turned gold into god,
whose lives are ruled by things they want
but that can't truly satisfy them.
Please, God, set us all free
when we find ourselves getting into that.*

---

* I often do it – but most of the time it's a typing error!

Mixed marriage, mixed monarchy

Based on the Book of Ruth

Now, I've got to ask it – just how much misfortune can one person handle? I mean, take Naomi, for example. Everything had seemed fine when she moved from Israel to Moab with her husband and two little boys. Even when her husband died, she managed to look after her sons, and when they grew up they married two women from Moab, called Ruth and Orpah, and things seemed to be good again. Then, the real disaster struck. Naomi's two sons died, as well. So there she was, in a foreign country, with no one in the world but her two daughters-in-law. And the trouble was that in those days it was really hard for a woman to earn a living – all the good jobs were for men, but there weren't any men in Naomi's family any more.

Then, Naomi heard that things were really good in Israel – there'd been a great harvest that year, and people had jobs and money again. 'Let's go back to Israel,' Naomi suggested.

On the way, though, Naomi realised it wasn't a case of 'back to Israel' for Ruth and Orpah – they were Moabites, and they were leaving their own country to be with her. 'Look,' she said, 'you stay in Moab – you're young, you're beautiful, and you'll have a good chance of marrying again. You're much better off here. Anyway, you know what my people can be like about Moabites – I hate to say it, but most of my people don't like yours at all. You'll have a rough time if you come with me.'

Orpah cried, kissed Naomi goodbye and turned back, but Ruth was determined. 'Look, here, Mum-in-law,' she said, 'I'm not giving up on you that easily – I'll go wherever you go. From now on, your people are my people, your

A story, a hug and a prayer

God is my God – and may God do his worst to me if I let you down. Got it?'

So it was that they arrived in Israel together. 'Just think,' said Naomi, sadly, 'I left here a rich woman, and I'm coming back as poor as a synagogue spider. We've got to find a way of earning a living.'

'Let me worry about that,' Ruth said. 'I'll go and be a gleaner* – it's not much but it'll be a living. I'll do that.'

Now, what do you think happened? Well, it turned out that Ruth was working in a field owned by a rich relation of Naomi's. Boaz was his name, and he was impressed – seriously impressed. 'Who's that woman working in the field?' he asked his manager.

'Oh, just some Moabite,' replied the other. 'Ruth, a friend of Naomi. Tell you what – she's a good worker.'

Boaz went over to speak to Ruth. 'Stay in this field,' he said, 'and I'll make sure no one bothers you. And if you want a drink, just ask – now, what are you doing for lunch?'

So it was that Boaz and Ruth began to get to know each other – and it wasn't long before Naomi caught on. 'Boaz!' she exclaimed. 'He's a relation of mine – rich, and kind with it, and that's a combination you don't often find.'

Time went by, and Naomi decided she'd better give events a bit of help. 'Boaz will be working late tonight, and he'll probably sleep in the barn,' she told Ruth. 'Now go and get yourself dolled up – nothing obvious, mind, he doesn't go for that sort of thing – and just go and lie down near to him so that when he wakes up he finds you there. If he can't take a hint like that, then he's really got a problem!'

So, when Boaz woke up the next morning, he could smell beautiful perfume. 'Well,' he thought, 'either I'm starting a new trend in male fashions, or there's a woman here.' And of course there was. And of course, it worked.

Boaz was a perfect gentleman. 'You'd better slip out of here,' he said, 'before people get the wrong idea. Look,

---

* Ask if the children know what gleaners did? They went behind the reapers at harvest time, picking up the corn they dropped.

Mixed marriage, mixed monarchy

according to our laws, Naomi's nearest relative is supposed to provide for you – so I've got to give him the chance. If he doesn't want to, then the way's clear for us to be married. Let me talk to him first – with a bit of luck he'll give us his blessing.'

And that's how it happened that Ruth, a Moabite, a member of the race that most Israelites really hated, showed how love and kindness can break down even the worst of bad feelings.

And that's not the end of the story. After they were married, Ruth became a mother – and then a grandmother – and then a great-grandmother. And who do you think her great-grandson was? A chap called David – remember him, the shepherd boy turned giant-killer, turned king of all Israel. And all because Ruth had loved Naomi enough to stick with her!

A story, a hug and a prayer

Let's chat . . .

*A lot of Naomi's people hated Moabites
just for being Moabites.
But God thought one of them was good enough
to be King David's great-great-grandmother!
Isn't it time we stopped putting labels on people
and got to know them instead?*

We're sad . . .

*Loving God, we're sorry
that we aren't always loving, like you.
However hard we try not to,
we do sometimes judge others unkindly
without really knowing them.
Please help us to be more open-minded.*

We're glad . . .

*Thank you, God, for difference!
Thank you that we aren't all the same!
Thank you for blue eyes, and brown eyes,*
for dark skin and fair skin.
Thank you for a wonderful, varied creation!*

Let's pray for people . . .

*Lord Jesus, please bless all people
who suffer unfairly because they're different.
Help them to know that they belong in your world
and help us to show that, in the way we treat them.*

---

* What colour are yours?

Brains before brawn

Based on 1 Samuel 25:1-35

Nabal was one of those guys you just couldn't please. You know the sort of thing – if you help them you're interfering and if you don't you've got no consideration. In short, he was a grouch. And that's not surprising because that's what his name – Nabal – actually meant.

Now, don't ask me how, but he'd got himself married to the sweetest, cleverest, most beautiful woman you could ever imagine. Abigail, her name was, and she had a brain to match her beauty – which was a good thing because as far as anyone could tell, Nabal had a brain to match *his* beauty, and that was a totally different matter. No one actually knew whether he'd never had one, or whether he'd lost it in a card game, but there was certainly no sign of it now – as became even more obvious when he came in from the farm one day, moaning and stamping his feet. 'That David,' he said, 'he only had the front to ask me to give him and his gang some food. Does he think I'm made of money?'

'I hope you weren't rude to him,' Abigail said, 'because I hear he's got a quick temper – and a lot of friends.'

'Rude? Me?' replied Nabal. 'Not at all – I just sent him a message saying he wouldn't get any food from me until he'd boiled his own head in a mustard sauce.'

Abigail was hopping mad. 'You said what? I hope you were joking. More to the point, I hope he *knows* you were joking!'

Nabal wasn't joking – you need wits to be witty, so Nabal never joked. 'Load of scroungers,' he said, 'no homes, no jobs, on the run from the king – just because Saul's gone mad and started killing everyone who disagrees with him is

A story, a hug and a prayer

no reason to run away. As far as I'm concerned, David's bad news.'

'Oh, yes, of course,' answered Abigail. 'Really bad news, when he and his friends have helped with the harvest, guarded your sheep and kept poachers away from your land – yes, I can see how you don't want anything like that happening, you brain-dead, intellectually challenged earthworm!'

Meanwhile, back at his camp, David was just receiving Nabal's message. 'Right, men,' he shouted. 'The first 400 to get their swords on, come with me – the rest can guard the camp. We're finally going to find out where Nabal's brain is – we're going to take him apart and look for it.'

Well, everybody hated Nabal, so in no time at all David and 400 friends were riding out of the camp toward Nabal's house.

Which, of course, is exactly what Abigail guessed would be happening. She started giving orders to her servants. 'Get me some donkeys,' she said. 'No, not Nabal – some intelligent ones. And lots of presents – wine, figs, bread, meat, grain – as much as you can find. It's time for some serious peace-making.'

Very soon, Abigail was riding out to meet David. Just imagine it: 401 men, with sharp swords, long spears and fierce tempers, against one woman with a load of groceries. Hardly seems promising, does it?

When Abigail saw David and his men coming, she stopped and dismounted, and put on her sweetest smile. Now, that would have stopped a cruise missile in full flight, so David had no chance. He stopped, and Abigail *really* turned on the charm.

'Oh, sir, I'm really sorry about that dreadful husband of mine. Of course, if he were bright and handsome and thoughtful like you, he'd never have said those things. Can you ever forgive us?'

'*Of course* I forgive you,' David beamed at her. 'Thank God I met you before I got to Nabal, because believe me there'd have been some blood flowing – and all over one bad-tempered old grouch.'

Brains before brawn

'Well,' Abigail smiled sweetly, 'one thing you can say about my husband – he always lives down to his name. Now, I've got to get back before he picks a fight with his own shadow – and loses. Enjoy the food and the wine.'

When Abigail got back, Nabal was all geared up for action, standing at the gate with three farmhands armed with pitchforks, like some former-day Dad's Army. 'It's all right,' Abigail told them. 'The battle's over. Everybody won.'

A story, a hug and a prayer

Let's chat . . .

Know someone like Nabal?
I guess most of us do!
The question is, do we meet them on their own level
– and make things worse –
or on God's
– and turn evil to good?

We're sad . . .

If we're honest, God,
we can all be 'Nabal' at times.
Some of us actually do it rather well!
Please help us to be kinder.

We're glad . . .

We've really got to say thank you, God,
for people like Abigail.
Please help us to learn her ways
of turning enemies into friends.

Let's pray for people . . .

Some very powerful people
behave like Nabal, too.
Please guide politicians
and help them to make peace
rather than leap to war.

Prophet and loss

Based on 1 Kings 17:8-24

Can you imagine having just enough food for one last meal – and knowing that after that you're going to starve to death? I can't – let's hope we never know what that's like – but let me introduce you to two people who know exactly how it feels.

Imagine the scene: close your eyes, and we're going back in time – back, back, to before anyone we know was born . . . back to the time when Jesus was born, but we're not stopping; back even further to – oh, there's King Solomon building the temple – we've gone too far. Forward a bit: that's it – about, oh, eight or nine hundred years before Jesus was born. We're a little way off from the place that happened, too – in Zarephath, just outside Israel. It's really hot – I mean, so hot that nothing will grow. And a widow called Anna and her son Joe are going to have that last meal I mentioned.

So, there's Anna, out gathering sticks for firewood, when she sees this weird-looking guy. He's sitting on the ground to take the weight off his blistered feet, and his clothes look as though he's hiked across a desert in them – probably because he has. 'Excuse me, missus,' he says to her, 'but I could really murder a drink. Got a bit of water, have you?'

Now, remember, there's been no rain for yonks, so water's like gold – well, better, actually: what use is gold when you're thirsty? Still, Anna thinks, they're going to die anyway, so why not help this poor old man?

'Yes, OK – I'll go and get you a drop,' she says. Then as she walks away, she can't believe her ears.

'A nice bit of bread would be cool,' the man calls out.

A story, a hug and a prayer

Anna turns round. 'Bread!' she repeats, incredulously. 'Bread! Look, mister, I've got just enough flour left to mix with about three drops of olive oil that's left in the bottle, and I'm going to make a last meal for Joe and me – Joe's my boy – and then we're going to die of starvation. Give you bread? I think not, somehow!'

'Right,' says the man, 'I'll tell you what. I'm a prophet, see – holy man – me and God, we're sort of close, you know. And he's promising that if you do this thing for me your flour jar will never run out, and there'll always be olive oil in the bottle until the end of the water shortage. So, how about it?'

Well, I ask you – here's this guy with his clothes in tatters and his feet growing fungus, who's obviously forgotten what water feels like on the skin, telling her he's God's agent and this is her big break. Would you believe him?

OK, but for some reason, Anna *does* believe him – and the next thing she knows she's making this bread from the flour and oil and sitting down to eat it with her son, Joe, and – oh, did I tell you the prophet's name was Elijah? Well, that's put that right, now, hasn't it.

But, you know, it's amazing. After that, every time Anna goes to look for flour, she finds some in the jar. And every time she uses that last drop of olive oil from the bottle, some more appears. 'This is unbelievable!' she says. 'You're obviously a good sort to have around.'

Well, things go on OK for a while, but then Joe gets ill. I mean, really ill – like I hope you'll never be – probably the heat and the water shortage that did it, but no one really knows. Anyway, nothing they do can save him, and he dies. 'Oh, I get it!' Anna screams at Elijah. 'This is what comes of having a holy man under my roof – you've reminded God of something I did wrong and he's punishing me for it by killing my child.' Well, don't be too hard on her – there are still people around even today who think that God does that kind of thing.

Anyway, Elijah doesn't argue – just says, 'Give the boy to me,' and takes him and lays him on his own bed. Then he prays like he's never prayed before. 'Hey, God, what's the story? I mean, just what d'you think you're doing? This woman's been really kind to me, and you go and do a horrible thing like this to her?' Then he prays, 'O God, give the lad his life back!' Nothing happens, so he says it again. Still nothing. Three times, he has to say it – three! – and suddenly, Joe starts breathing again. So Elijah gets him off the bed and straight downstairs to his mother. 'Hey,' he says, 'have I got news for you – here he is!'

Well, if Anna thought the flour and the oil were something, she's got to be *seriously* impressed by this! 'No doubt about it,' she says, 'you're a man of God all right – I mean, why God should want to work through someone with your dress sense, I don't really know – but he obviously does.'

A story, a hug and a prayer

Let's chat . . .

*Amazing – Anna being so kind to Elijah
when she had so little!
But it's often the poorest people
who are the most generous
– perhaps because they know
that they need one another.*

We're sad . . .

*We've got so much,
compared with some other people!
Please forgive us, God, if sometimes
we're unkind or selfish.
Help us to remember how much
we need each other.*

We're glad . . .

*Thank you, God, for all our friends,
all the people who love us.
Thank you for the chances we have
to show your love
by being kind to others.*

Let's pray for people . . .

*We pray for people who are really poor,
people who are so hungry it hurts.
We pray for charities like Christian Aid
and all who try to find real, permanent answers
to the problem of poverty.
Please help us to do our part
in supporting them.*

Elijah listens and learns

Based on 1 Kings 19:1-21

Poor Elijah's back on the run. He's just upset wicked Queen Jezebel – again – and, not for the first time, he takes to his toes and makes for the hills – runs as if his life depends upon it (which, of course, it does). To cut a slightly longer story short, he ends up at a cave in the mountains. 'No one'll find me here,' he thinks. 'I'll get a bit of peace.'

Wrong, Elijah! There's one person who'll find you, wherever you are – and what's going to happen to you now is hardly peaceful! So, who's the person who can find you wherever you are – apart from the truant officer, that is? Well, it's God, isn't it? So Elijah's just thinking he's got the place to himself when he hears this voice. 'Hey, Elijah! What are you doing here?'

Elijah can hardly believe God's asking him such a silly question. 'What am I doing here?' he says. 'Look, I've done all right by you, haven't I? I mean, I've really tried – but what have the people of Israel done? Broken all their promises, that's what – not to mention smashing up all your worship places. Oh, yes, and they've killed all your prophets, too – I'm the only friend you've got left in the world, and now they're after me. I think the reason I'm hiding here might be just a touch obvious, don't you?'

Now, I guess God might have been a bit sad about that – I mean, there have always been people who thought they were the only friend God had, but he'd probably hoped Elijah would know better. 'Go and stand at the cave entrance,' he tells Elijah. 'And whatever happens, you stay there, OK – because I'm going to be passing that way and you just might learn something.'

A story, a hug and a prayer

So, Elijah goes to stand just inside the mouth of the cave. He's hardly got there when there's this huge hurricane. I mean, huge enough to break rocks into little bits – have *you* ever seen wind do that? Great big rocks are flying past the cave entrance and breaking into little fragments. Naturally, Elijah thinks God must be in the wind – but not a word does he hear. Nothing at all.

Next, it's an earthquake – everything's shaking like a jelly at a children's party, and Elijah thinks God must be in the earthquake. But he's not. Then comes a fire – seems as if the whole world's going up in smoke: great clouds of soot and ash falling around the mouth of the cave, but no sign of God anywhere.

Elijah's just about had enough, by now. He doesn't know what God's trying to pull, but he'd have had less trouble if he'd stayed where Queen Jezebel could find him. 'Well,' he thinks, 'if God passed by I must've missed him.' And he turns to go back. But what d'you think happens next?

Next, he hears nothing at all. Just silence – a really eerie silence – the kind where you just know that something's waiting to happen. So Elijah wraps his cloak round his head, creeps to the front of the cave entrance and peers out. It's so quiet, not even the leaves on the trees are rustling, and Elijah's sure something big's about to go off – that God's going to show himself, now, and it's going to be even more spectacular than everything that's just happened all put together. Very gingerly, he steps out of the cave on to the mountainside. Then it happens. The voice is really quiet, so he can hardly hear it, but he knows jolly well who it is. 'Elijah,' God whispers, 'what are you doing here?'

Well, that sets Elijah off again. 'I've been really good,' he says, 'really enthusiastic – you know? I've done everything you asked me to, but they've been and gone and ignored you – there's not an altar or a prophet standing upright in the whole country, except me. I'm the only friend you've got left, and they're after me, too. Hey, haven't we been through this before?'

'Go home, Elijah,' God says to him. 'On the way, you'll

Elijah listens and learns

meet a few other friends of mine, like Hazael and Jehu – they're going to be kings – and a guy called Elisha who's going to be a prophet. He doesn't know it yet, but he will. Now, it's going to turn nasty – I won't lie to you about that – but there'll be another 7000 friends of mine left to pick up the pieces, so you're hardly the last one, are you?'

So off goes Elijah, finds this Elisha chap and sets him up as his own servant – well, young prophets have to start at the bottom, you know. He's got a lot to learn, but he'll have a good teacher. Elijah's a much wiser man, now.

A story, a hug and a prayer

Let's chat . . .

Just listen to Elijah!
'I'm the only friend you've got left.'
I mean, come on!
Is it likely God would ever be that low on friends?
How often have we said,
'No one understands me – I'm all alone'?
There are more good people out there
than we give God credit for.

We're sad . . .

Sorry for not trusting you enough, God.
Just that sometimes it really does feel
as if we're all alone in the world.
Then we start feeling sorry for ourselves.
Please help us remember
that you never let things get that bad.

We're glad . . .

Thank you, God, for all those good people
who are standing up for truth and for goodness
even when the things going on around us
lead us to forget them.
Thank you for loving, caring people.

Let's pray for people . . .

Some of those good people
are in very dangerous places,
because they choose to be there.
Thank you for people who take aid to war zones,
or face danger to rescue people in trouble.
Please bless all unselfish people
and let them know that they're appreciated.

I may be little, but I matter

Based on 1 Kings 21

One day, King Ahab looked out of his palace window and thought: 'I could really use that vineyard next door. I could grow vegetables in it.' So, next time he saw Naboth, his neighbour, in his vineyard, Ahab went and leant on the fence, the way you do, for a bit of a natter.

'Nice day, Naboth,' he said, chattily.

'I suppose so,' Naboth answered, warily. Ahab only ever bothered to be friendly if he wanted something.

'Just the day for doing a bit of veggie-gardening,' Ahab answered. 'Can't beat a good organic carrot, can you?'

'I suppose not,' Naboth repeated, 'but why would anybody want to beat a carrot? Now, eggs, I could understand.'

'Of course,' Ahab continued, 'you need the right land for it, and yours would be perfect. So, why don't you let me have it? I'll give you another plot somewhere else – or if you like, I'll just pay you for it.'

Naboth didn't even stop to consider it. 'No,' he said.

'Sorry, I don't understand,' King Ahab responded.

'No,' Naboth repeated. 'This was my family's land – my granddad gave it to my dad, and he gave it to me. Now, that sort of thing matters to people like me, and I'm not selling.'

King Ahab was amazed. People didn't normally use words like 'No' to him. He was so upset that he went home to his palace, lay on his bed and sulked.

'Now, what's the matter with you,' Queen Jezebel asked him. 'You look as though you've swallowed a dung-beetle.'

'Naboth won't sell me his land,' Ahab whined.

'Oh, won't he, now – what does he think he is? Important

A story, a hug and a prayer

or something? Look, are you king around here, or aren't you?'

Jezebel hatched a cunning plot. She got a good crowd of witnesses together, and then bribed a couple of liars to do what they did best – lie through their teeth.

'Naboth cursed God,' one of them said.

'Yes,' added the other. 'And he cursed the king, too!'

'It's true,' said the first. 'We both heard him.'

'Oh, no I never!' Naboth protested.

'Oh, yes, you did,' said one of the liars.

'We both heard you,' the other one added, 'and there are two of us to one of you.'

Poor Naboth! He never stood a chance! The crowd grabbed hold of him and dragged him through the streets toward the city wall.

'I tell you, I didn't do it!' Naboth continued to protest. 'I'm a loyal subject of the king, I am – even if he does want to take my land off me – oh, I get it!'

He did, too – just as soon as they got him out of the city, he got it. It's not a nice way to die, having a crowd throw stones at you – especially when you know you don't deserve it.

Before long, Jezebel got a message to say Naboth was dead. 'You can go and take a walk in *your* vineyard, now,' she said to Ahab. 'That jumped-up little Naboth person has got what was coming to him.'

Now, Ahab must have been suspicious – wouldn't you have been? But he just went down the garden and into Naboth's vineyard as though he'd bought it fair and square.

He hadn't been there long when he saw someone he didn't want to see. God had sent Elijah, the prophet, to set him straight about a few things. 'Oh-oh,' Ahab grunted, 'so you've found me, have you – my enemy.'

'Oh, yes,' Elijah answered. 'God sent me. You've really got his dander up, this time. And I'm here to tell you you're not going to get away with it.'

Now, I'm not going to put you off your sleep by going into the details, but let's just say that Ahab ended up very sorry about what had happened to Naboth – very sorry, indeed. And as for what became of Jezebel – well, that'll

I may be little, but I matter

keep for another time, too. But God left them in no doubt: ordinary people like Naboth might seem like small potatoes to a king or queen – but to God they're just as important as everyone else. And he loves them.

A story, a hug and a prayer

Let's chat . . .

Poor Naboth!
Telling the truth, but not believed
– all because he was outnumbered by liars!
It's an unfair world.

We're sad . . .

You know, God, it really makes us sad
– in fact it makes us cross, too –
that the world is sometimes so unfair!
Please help us not to add to that
in the way we treat one another.

We're glad . . .

Even though it's unfair, though,
this is your world.
And that means there's always lots of good in it, too.*
Help us to see the signs of your goodness,
and to celebrate them.

Let's pray for people . . .

We pray for people who suffer from unfairness.
Please, God, use us and other people
to show your love.
So that people can believe in your kindness
as well as in their own worth.

---

* Encourage the children to offer examples.

This isn't happening!

Based on 2 Kings 2:1-18

Elisha, the apprentice prophet, was in denial. He knew God was about to take his teacher, Elijah, up into heaven – and that's why Elisha, and a lot of other people, too, were behaving distinctly strangely.

Elijah was OK – a bit restless, perhaps, but OK. It was everybody else! The two men were on their way from Gilgal when Elijah said: 'You wait here. God's told me to go to Bethel.'

'What? Me – leave you? Not on your life!' Elisha answered. So that was that, and together they arrived at Bethel where some local prophets came to meet them – Elijah was a bit of a celebrity by the standards of the day.

Anyway, the prophets came out and said: 'Hey, Elisha, did you know that God's taking Elijah away today?'

'I know, I know!' Elisha answered. 'Just don't say anything to him – OK?'

Next, God sent Elijah to Jericho. 'You'd better stay here,' he told Elisha.

So, Elisha went with him. Another group of prophets met them at Jericho and had the same conversation with Elisha – which ended with Elisha telling them to keep the news to themselves.

Next stop was the Jordan. Again, Elijah told Elisha to stay put, and again Elisha piggy-backed on Elijah's shadow and stuck with him – and by now they'd got a whole trail of about 50 other prophets all tagging along to see the action. When they arrived at the Jordan, Elijah took his cloak and swiped the water with it. Elisha watched in amazement as the water parted, leaving a dry path for them to walk across.

A story, a hug and a prayer

The other prophets kept their distance. Everybody knew what was happening, but no one wanted really to believe it – no one, that is, except Elijah who seemed quite calm about the whole thing.

'Is there anything you want me to do for you?' he asked Elisha, 'before God takes me away?'

Elisha remembered the parted waters of the river. 'A double helping of whatever it is that you've got wouldn't go amiss,' he answered.

'Now, that's a tough one,' Elijah replied. 'Still, if you're around to see me taken away from you then you'll have it.'

They carried on talking as they walked. And then it happened. You know how it is when you can see something developing but can't do anything about it? Well, that's how it was for Elisha. Something was coming toward them, very quickly. It was incredibly bright and moving like a race-winning chariot. Actually, it *was* a chariot, but it was different – seemed to be on fire. As it came closer, Elisha could see that the whole chariot was ablaze. Then it came closer still, and he realised that it was actually *made* of fire – and so were the horses that were pulling it.

Elisha watched in fascination and amazement as the chariot came closer, closer, and – no, it's impossible, surely! – it went straight through between him and Elijah without even singeing their eyebrows!

Elisha had no time to reflect on it, though, because something else was coming – a hurricane! He could see the sand being stirred up and lifted into the air. Then he saw Elijah, standing quite calm and still as the hurricane picked him up without even ruffling his hair, and carried him toward heaven.

Elisha could do nothing but simply stand there and watch, calling out to Elijah as he did. 'My father! My father! It's the chariots and cavalry of Israel!'

Elisha stared at Elijah as if trying to hold him within his sight, but it was pointless. Elijah disappeared up to heaven, leaving Elisha really upset. Oh, he knew Elijah was safe, of course – he trusted God – but he was still going to miss him like crazy!

This isn't happening!

Elijah's cloak had fallen to the ground. Elisha picked it up and walked back to the Jordan where he swiped the water as Elijah had done. 'OK, so where's Elijah's God, now?' he shouted.

As if to answer, the water separated again, and Elisha walked across. The prophets were still there, standing at a distance. 'Elijah's spirit's in you now!' they said. But then they seemed to contradict themselves. 'We've got 50 good men,' they said. 'Let's send them to look for your boss!'

Elisha tried to stop them, but it was no good, so he eventually said: 'Oh, go if you must, then.' After three days they'd still not found him, and everyone finally had to admit that Elijah was gone. 'I told you so,' Elisha couldn't resist saying. 'I told you not to search. We've got to let Elijah go.'

Elijah had left Elisha a lot more than that old cloak, though. God worked through Elisha just as he had through Elijah, and made him into a truly great prophet.

A story, a hug and a prayer

Let's chat . . .

It's hard to say goodbye, isn't it?
Sometimes we have to leave friends
when we move house, school or work.
Sometimes we lose people for other reasons.
Of course we're unhappy – we're going to miss them.
But it's a little less hard if we trust God for the future.

We're sad . . .

Isn't it strange, God,
how we often don't really appreciate people
until we have to separate from them?
Please help us to appreciate all our friends.

We're glad . . .

Thank you for friends, Lord,
and thank you for your promise of new life.
Thank you for showing us that every ending
paves the way for a new beginning.

Let's pray for people . . .

Please, God, comfort people who are sad
because they've been separated from someone.
Help us always to be honest about our feelings,
and at the same time to trust you.

Healing Naaman's prejudices

Based on 2 Kings 5:1-14

This is the story of Naaman – a really powerful man. Naaman was the top soldier in Aram – in charge of the whole army. And he was doing well, too; his country was always quarrelling with their neighbour, Israel, and Naaman had fought lots of battles and won. So he was a real favourite of the king.

Just one problem: Naaman had a really nasty skin condition, and he used to get well embarrassed whenever he did a victory parade. Everybody was cheering him and saying what a great soldier he was, but he was convinced that they were pointing at him, too, and commenting on his terrible skin.

Now, on one of his raids into Israel, Naaman had captured a young girl and given her to his wife as a servant. You might think she'd be glad that Naaman was unhappy, but she wasn't – she actually felt really sorry for him. So one day, she said to Naaman's wife, 'You know, there's a prophet in Israel – well, Samaria, actually, but it amounts to the same thing – who could cure him of this.'

Well, anything seemed worth a try, so the king of Aram sent a letter to the king of Israel asking him to fix something up. The king of Israel didn't trust him, though. 'Oh, I get it!' he said. 'He asks me to cure his commander – knowing that I can't do any such thing – and when I fail he's got another excuse to send his army to attack me. Oh, what am I going to do?'

Of course, Naaman's king had written to the wrong guy – typical aristocrat: it didn't occur to him that ordinary folk can possibly be of any use! The man he really wanted was

A story, a hug and a prayer

Elisha, the prophet. Still, you know how it is when royals are in trouble – the word gets around very quickly, and in less time than it would take for a worm to ruin a perfectly good apple, Elisha had heard all about it. 'Send him to me,' he told the king. 'I'll show him who's God in this world.'

So, Naaman took lots of presents and money – and a troupe of servants to carry them all – and went to see Elisha. He knocked on the door and stood waiting for the great prophet to come out and do something spectacular to cure him. The door opened. 'Yes?' said a voice.

'I'm Naaman, victorious commander of the army of Aram – and I've come to see the prophet Elisha.'

'Wait 'ere,' said the servant, and he shut the door and disappeared! Now, this wasn't how Naaman was used to being treated. And it got worse when the servant reappeared and said, ''E says you're to go and wash seven times in the Jordan – that'll clean yer up.' And he was gone again, leaving Naaman staring at the closed door.

Naaman had never been more hopping mad, more beside himself with rage, more . . . oh, I don't know . . . in his entire life. 'I expected to see the prophet personally – face to face – one great man to another!' he raged. 'Who does he think he is, treating me like this? He's supposed to come out to me himself . . . say a well impressive prayer . . . invoke his God . . . wave his hands over me and cure the disease. I didn't come all this way for a wash; I can get one of those in the rivers of Damascus – they're better than this muddy little brook they call the Jordan, anyway. Come on, guys – we're going home.'

Now, Naaman's servants had a bit more sense than their master – which is not unusual, but that's another matter – and they had a word with him. 'Look, sir,' they said, 'if he'd asked you to do something really spectacular, you'd have done that, wouldn't you? So what harm can a simple wash in the river do you?'

Well, for all his faults, Naaman knew when someone was talking sense, so he decided to give it a go. No one said he had to enjoy it, though. He gingerly waded into the river

Healing Naaman's prejudices

until he was up to his waist, before he took a deep breath, held his nose and ducked under the water. Once . . . twice . . . three times . . . oh, this was so undignified! . . . four . . . five . . . six . . . oh, all right then, just one more . . . seven!

Naaman grumpily got out of the river and dried himself off. And it was then that he noticed. There were none of those little white flaky bits on the towel. He looked down and what d'you think he saw? Skin! Beautiful, healthy, young-looking skin. 'Well!' he said. 'It's a long time since I've seen that, except on other people!'

Naaman learnt a lot from that – about humility, and about the importance of little acts and ordinary people – but most of all about God. So it wasn't just his skin problem that got sorted out that day. Naaman went home a truly beautiful person – and it was more than skin deep.

A story, a hug and a prayer

Let's chat . . .

Most of us dream of doing great things,
rescuing someone from danger, perhaps,
or saving the world from disaster.
But if we were all busy doing great things,
who'd there be to do the 'ordinary' things
that keep life going for us?

We're sad . . .

We're good at daydreaming,
and getting big ideas.
Then we end up by not valuing the little things.
Please forgive us, God, for getting things out of proportion,
and teach us to value the ordinary stuff.

We're glad . . .

You know, Lord, it would be a terrible world
if it weren't for 'ordinary' people,
doing 'ordinary' things!
Thank you for people who are happy to do them!

Let's pray for people . . .

Some people are so unhappy, Lord,
because they want to be 'great' or 'famous'.
Some of them get their wish,
and sometimes they seem even unhappier!
We pray for all people who are unhappy
with who they are, or what they do.
Please help us all to value each other
and ourselves, too!

God has hidden depths

Based on the book of Jonah

Jonah was saying his prayers – but they were unusual prayers, because he wasn't at all happy with God. 'I don't believe it!' he stormed. 'You want me to go to Nineveh, and preach? You want me to save a bunch of foreigners! Aren't there any of your own people that need saving?'

'*All* people are my people, Jonah,' God said, sternly.

'Well, yes, in theory – but you know what I mean. Haven't we got enough problems here for me to sort out, without sending me off to save a crowd of aliens?'

'Seems to me,' God said, 'that you need your mind broadening more than somewhat – and a bit of travel will help. Subject closed. You're to go to Nineveh.'

So that's how Jonah came to be at the Joppa docks, looking for a boat. 'Hmm,' he thought. 'So God wants me to travel, does he? Well, all these boats look so much the same, he can't blame me if I accidentally get on the one for Spain, can he?'

Now, that was a bad idea – a *seriously* bad idea, as Jonah found out as soon as the boat got out to sea. He was having a bit of a doze in the ship's hold when the captain woke him up. The boat was pitching all over the place in the biggest storm Jonah had ever known. Even the captain was terrified: 'Don't just lie there – get praying,' barked the old sea-dog. 'Everyone else is.'

'Oh, of course – God!' thought Jonah. 'Funny how he always seems to know where I am! OK, OK – no need for the "You can run but you can't hide" speech – I'll own up.'

So Jonah told the captain everything, and finished up by saying, 'If you throw me overboard, then it'll stop.'

65

A story, a hug and a prayer

Well, they tried everything else. They threw most of the cargo away to lighten the ship, but that just made it easier for the sea to throw it around. Eventually, they had to do it. So over the side Jonah went, and right down into the depths of the sea. Gradually, his eyes got used to it, and he saw that he was heading towards a big cave. 'I don't fancy that very much,' he thought, and began to swim for the surface – but to his amazement, the cave followed. The faster he swam, the faster the cave came toward him.*

Then he realised – it wasn't a cave, but the mouth of the biggest fish he'd ever seen. And before he could say, 'No salt on my chips, please,' it had caught him.

Now, there's something about being in a fish's stomach that makes you think, don't you think? You don't know? Well, try and keep it that way. Fishes' stomachs are not nice places for people to end up. Jonah thought it was probably time he and God got their friendship back on a proper footing.

'Thanks, God,' he said. 'I thought I was a goner that time, but you saved me. Now, I've got to get out of this, one way or another, and either way it's not going to be very nice. Still, if you help me, I'll help you – well, it's only fair, isn't it? I'll serve you really well – not like those nasty foreigners. I'll do whatever you say.'

'Well, you can start with Nineveh,' said God. 'and less of the nasty foreigners stuff, if you know what's good for you.' Then he spoke to the fish. 'OK, Jonesey – full ahead to dry land, and thanks for your co-operation. Nice to know there are some creatures I can rely on.'

This time, Jonah did as God said. He went to Nineveh, and he preached. Everyone changed the way they were living and God decided not to punish them after all.

'I knew it!' Jonah stormed. 'Rotten lot of foreigners – and now you've been kind to them. Sometimes, I just don't understand you at all.'

'Well, you got that one right,' said God. 'You look a bit

---

* Any idea what it really was?

God has hidden depths

hot – how about a nice tree for some shade?' Immediately, a tree grew up to shelter Jonah from the sun. Jonah was really pleased – until the next day, when God killed the tree and Jonah got hot under the collar – and everywhere else – again.

'Wha – what did you do that for?' he raved at God. 'Fancy killing a poor little tree.'

'Oh, I see,' God answered. 'You feel sorry for a tree, but you want me to destroy a city of 120,000 people – not to mention the animals – just to satisfy your prejudice. I think it's time you got your priorities straight, don't you?'

A story, a hug and a prayer

Let's chat . . .

Who did Jonah think he was?!
He was a man with serious prejudices, wasn't he?
Just a minute, though:
don't we sometimes feel like that?
Haven't we ever been so angry with people
that we want to see them punished, not changed?
I know I feel that way too often.
I'm not proud of it – but I can't deny it.

We're sad . . .

Please forgive us, God,
for letting our anger and our prejudice
get the better of us.
Help us to want only good for other people.

We're glad . . .

There are some people who never seem to hold a grudge,
and who only want what's best for others
– even for 'bad' others!
They really get to us, Lord –
that kind of goodness can be seriously irritating.
But thank you for them, anyway!

Let's pray for people . . .

We pray for people who feel spiteful,
and make themselves unhappy.
Please help them find happiness
in being more generous of spirit.
Oh, and by the way, God:
can you include us, too,
when we feel that way?

Peter goes over the top

Based on Matthew 14:22-33

Have you ever had one of those times when you suddenly found you could do something you couldn't do before? Great, isn't it – you feel on top of the world. The trouble is – if you're anything like me – you can easily be carried away and get a bit careless. And that's when things get . . . well . . . interesting isn't quite a strong enough word for it.

So, imagine the scene. There's Peter – one of Jesus' disciples – out in a boat with the rest of the gang. Jesus isn't there, because he's stayed behind to get a bit of quiet time with God, saying he'll catch them up later.

'I don't know how he thinks he's going to catch up with us,' Peter says to Andrew. 'We'll be across the lake long before he could ever walk round it.'

'Well, you never know,' his brother Andrew jokes. 'Maybe he's going to walk straight across – anything can happen, with Jesus.'

'I'm serious!' Peter objects. 'I'm a fisherman and I reckon I know more about boats and sailing and all that stuff than a carpenter does – even if the carpenter's Jesus.'

Just then, James cuts in. 'You'd better stop the silly talk and get working,' he says. 'There's a storm coming.'

He's right, too. The sky's darkening and there's a wind whistling through the gap in the hills and stirring up the surface of the lake. They just about have time to get the sail down and stowed away, and then it hits them – with a force like they've never known before. The boat's tossing and pitching all over the place – much too far from land for them to get back – and water's washing in over the side faster than they can throw it back out. They know they're

A story, a hug and a prayer

in real trouble. Isn't it just the way? When you really need a saviour there's never one around!

Or is there? Andrew's staring back toward the land with his mouth open and his eyes on stalks. 'Hey!' Peter yells. 'This is no time to freeze – it's the time to panic! Grab a bucket and start baling out the water.'

Andrew points. 'What's that?' They follow his trembling finger and see something that frightens them sillier than the storm does: it looks like a man walking along on the top of the water. Now, Andrew had thought that idea was a good joke before, but it doesn't seem funny, now!

'It's a ghost!' says Philip. 'That's what it must be – a living person couldn't do that.'

'Maybe it's coming for us!' James' voice is trembling at the very idea.

Then the figure calls out to them. 'Hey, you guys, get a grip – it's me!'

Is it? It can't be! It is, though: it's Jesus himself, walking along on the top of the waves as if everybody does it all the time.

Now, you remember what I said about learning new tricks? Well, that bit's just coming. And the bit about being carried away and getting into trouble? That's coming up, too. Anyway, as far as we know no one else has ever done this, so I don't think I'd try it if I were you.

Now, where was I? Oh, yes. This is where Peter has his *big idea*. 'Is it really you, Lord?' he shouts out. 'If it is, just say the word and I'll come to meet you.'

'Come on, then,' comes the reply, and Peter's out of that boat in a trice and walking along the top of the water toward Jesus. Then it suddenly dawns on him what he's doing. It's impossible! You can't walk on water! Try to walk on water, and you drown! So, next thing he knows he's up to his neck in water and blind panic, heading for a close encounter with a shoal of herrings.

It's horrible! Water's coming up over his head, and he soon won't be able to open his mouth without getting a salty drink. So, while he can still do it he yells out at the

Peter goes over the top

top of his voice, 'Save me, Lord! Heeeeeeelp!' Jesus acts quickly – reaches out a hand, grabs him and pulls him back up. 'You know your trouble?' he says. 'No faith – why were you all getting so panicky, just now?'

It's the most extraordinary thing, though: as soon as Jesus gets into the boat the wind stops. The disciples finally get the message. 'You're really something, you are, Jesus!' they say. 'Son of God, that's what.'

Mind you, just because they've said that, it won't stop them getting frightened and panicky next time they're in difficulties. Knowing's one thing – really trusting . . . well, that's something else, isn't it!

A story, a hug and a prayer

Let's chat . . .

Who are the people in our lives
that we really trust?
It's easy to talk about,
but much harder to do!
What would we trust these people with?
And what wouldn't we?

We're sad . . .

Please forgive us, Jesus,
when we don't really trust you enough,
when we get into a state about things
and act is if you're not around.
Help us to be more trusting.

We're glad . . .

Some people trust you, Jesus,
so much that they really change things.
Thank you for that kind of faith!

Let's pray for people . . .

Thank you, God,
for people who show real faith,
and who use that faith
to change the world around them.

Forgiven and unforgiving

Based on Matthew 18:21-34

'I'll kill him!' Peter was yelling. 'If Andrew criticises my fishing just once more . . . That's the sixth time he's done it today.'

'All I said,' Andrew protested, 'was that he couldn't fish for compliments.'*

'That's it! shouted Peter. 'That's seven times – and I reckon forgiving anybody seven times is enough, don't you, Jesus?'

'Not by a long chalk,' Jesus replied. 'In fact I'd say more like, oh, let's see, seventy times seven.'

Peter was amazed. 'Seventy times seven? Well, that's . . . that's . . . well, it's a lot, anyway.'

'Four hundred and ninety, actually,' Matthew replied. 'Trust me – I'm an accountant.'

Peter had a very quick answer ready for that, but Jesus interrupted. 'God's way of doing things is like this,' he said. 'Imagine a great king – right? And he's got this servant who owes him a lot of money.'

'How much money?' Matthew asked. 'We've got to get these details right, you know.'

'Oh, let's say ten grand,' Jesus answered.

'Ten grand!' Andrew whistled.

'About a quarter of a million crispy cod burgers, at today's

---

* Have you ever heard someone do that? Most of us have done it, perhaps by saying things like: 'Oh, I'm not very good at so-and-so,' just hoping someone will say: 'Oh, but you're brilliant at it.' Or we might say: 'I wish I were intelligent,' to which the hoped-for reply is: 'But you're *highly* intelligent'!

A story, a hug and a prayer

prices,' Mary Magdalene chipped in – 'more if you have them without batter.'

Jesus looked patient. 'Do you want to hear this story or not?'

'Sorry Jesus,' Peter apologised. 'I'm agog.'

'Exactly,' Andrew cut in. 'And gogs can't fish!'

'Are you going to listen?' said Jesus. 'Or shall I go down to the sea and talk to the waves, instead? Now, if I have your attention, this slave – we'll call him Simon – he owed the king all this money and the king wanted it back.'

'I don't blame him,' said Matthew.

'With knobs on,' agreed Mary.

'So he called Simon,' Jesus went on, 'and said: "I want my money." Of course, he knew Simon hadn't even got the price of a pair of shoelaces, let alone ten grand. "Don't worry, Simon," he said. "You needn't pay." Then, just as Simon was breathing a big sigh of relief, he added, "I'll just sell you instead – and your wife and children, and your belongings."

'Well,' Jesus went on, 'Simon begged and he pleaded – you've never seen anything like it since that sending off at the Jerusalem sports stadium last year, remember? Well, Simon grovelled, and he cried, and kissed the king's feet and said he'd get the money somehow.'

'Yeah, yeah,' Matthew scoffed, 'we've all heard that one before.'

Jesus glared. 'Are you telling this story, or am I? Anyway, the king was a kind old character, really, so he forgave him. "You needn't pay me," he said, "Just forget about it." '

'I say,' said Andrew, 'What a nice king!'

'A very nice king,' agreed Mary.

'Don't get carried away,' grunted Andrew. 'It only happens in books.'

'I've not finished yet,' Jesus said. 'Simon went running off to tell his wife the good news, and on the way he met another servant who owed him the price of a bag of cod tails.'

'They're ten a penny,' Mary cut in.

'Well,' Jesus continued, 'you'd have thought it was millions, the way Simon grabbed him, and shook him, and demanded

Forgiven and unforgiving

his money. Of course, the poor guy hadn't got it on him, so Simon had him put in prison and kept there until he paid everything.

'When the king found out, he was furious. "I let you off a debt of ten grand," he reminded Simon, "and now you've been and gone and done this to one of your own mates over a bag of cod-tails! Into prison you go until you've paid the ten grand." And he had him thrown into the cell.'

'Too right!' said Andrew.

'Deserved all he got,' Peter added.

'Ungrateful little wretch!' hissed Mary Magdalene.

'Fine,' Jesus smiled. 'So does this mean I can expect you lot to be civil to one another from now on?'

A story, a hug and a prayer

Let's chat . . .

It's a strange thing, forgiveness!
Does it undo whatever was done?
Does it make a bad action OK?
No? So what does it do?
Perhaps its real value is that it heals our relationships,
so the bad things we do don't make us fall out.

We're sad . . .

Forgiveness is too easy to talk about, Jesus,
and too hard to do!
Sometimes we say it but don't mean it,
and sometimes we expect it
just to get ourselves off the hook!
Help us to care for one another,
with all our faults.

We're glad . . .

When you think about it, God,
we've all been forgiven lots of times.
We must have been,
or we wouldn't have any friends left!
Thank you for friends and family
who love us enough to go on forgiving us!

Let's pray for people . . .

You know, God, it seems to us
that if we hold grudges against people,
the ones who really suffer are ourselves!
We can be so unhappy, always remembering
the bad things people have done.
So we pray for people who struggle to forgive,
so that they can find happiness.

You mean you didn't even try?

Based on Matthew 25:14-30

D'you know what a talent is – do you know what people mean when they say: 'She's got a talent for singing'? I'm going to tell you how the word came to be used that way. It started with a story Jesus told, at a time when 'talent' meant a kind of money – like a pound or a dollar.

Bart was a rich man. He had a big business empire, selling everything from nails to nutcrackers, from feathers to furniture. Most things people wanted, Bart could provide – which was why he was rich.

Bart had to go away for a while, and thought it a good chance for some of his staff to show what they could do. So he called three of them to him. John was very bright, and could probably handle quite a big project. 'You can have five talents,' Bart told him.

'Five talents!' John exclaimed. 'That's a lifetime's wages, to me. And I know just what to do with it.'

Then, Bart turned to Sarah. 'You can have two talents. With your imagination you should do well with that.'

Meanwhile, the third servant, Sam, was getting really worried. 'I don't want the responsibility,' he thought to himself. 'I'd rather stay as I am, thank you very much.'

'You can have one talent,' Bart said. 'I know you're not particularly energetic, but see what you can do with it.'

John wasted no time. He knew exactly where the opportunity lay. Bart's business sold most things people wanted, but John knew there were a lot of people who couldn't walk very well, or couldn't carry heavy things home. So he took on a team of people. 'Go out into the villages,' he said, 'and make a list of housebound people. Then you can visit them regularly, and take their orders.'

A story, a hug and a prayer

Well, in no time at all, things were really buzzing. John had found a whole new group of people to sell to. And it gave the company a good image, too, so other people who didn't need John's delivery service still shopped at Bart's because they liked to deal with a caring company.

Sarah had always wished she'd got a bit of money, because she wanted to invent something. Her mum, Mary, was getting old and her hands were weak. She'd always loved oranges, but now she couldn't enjoy them any more unless someone else peeled them for her – and always asking for help was embarrassing. Sarah knew there must be other people like her mum, and could see a market for a really good orange peeler for people with weak hands. Well, this was her chance. She spent her two talents on developing her idea, taking each new version of the peeler home for her mother to try. After months of patient work, she'd got it right and Mary was back to enjoying her favourite fruit again. Sarah had just enough money left from her two talents to start production of her new orange peeler, and before she knew what was happening, John's sales team were coming in with orders for it from all the surrounding villages. Sarah had a winner on her hands.

And what of Sam – what was he doing with his one talent? 'Huh!' he thought. 'I don't want any part of this. I know what'll happen – it'll all go wrong and then I'll get the blame because I couldn't live up to Bart's high standards. Well, I'm not getting involved. I'll just keep the money safe.' So Sam dug a hole and put the money in it, to wait for Bart to come home.

'Well,' said Bart, 'what have you done with your talents?'

John beamed with pride. 'Here are your five talents – and five talents profit from my new scheme.'

'Wonderful!' Bart exclaimed. 'I'll make you a partner in my business! What about you, Sarah?'

Sarah was proud, too. 'Here are your two talents back,' she said, 'and two more – profits from my invention.'

'Great stuff!' Bart congratulated her. 'I'm making you a partner in my business, too.'

You mean you didn't even try?

So what about Sam? Poor Sam! 'Well, it's like this,' he faltered. 'I, er, I knew what a great businessman you are – what high standards you set – and I didn't want to let you down. So I kept your money safe by burying it, and here's your one talent back.'

Bart was sad. 'Even if you failed,' he said, 'you could at least have tried. If nothing else, you could have put the money in the bank and got some interest. I'm really disappointed in you, Sam.'

Bart threw a party for John and Sarah, to celebrate their success. Poor Sam had nothing to celebrate, so he got left out. And that was a shame, because Bart wouldn't have punished him if he'd tried and failed. What hurt Bart was that Sam didn't trust him enough to take the risk.

A story, a hug and a prayer

Let's chat . . .

Poor Sam!
So afraid of failure that he didn't even try!
Of course, we all have to 'walk before we can run',
but let's at least try to walk!

We're sad . . .

We're sorry, God,
for not trusting you.
Deep down, we know you love us,
whether we succeed or not,
but we don't always act on that.
Help us to trust you more.

We're glad . . .

Thank you, God,
for being the kind of God you are!
Thank you for loving, and loving and loving!
Thank you for showing your love in people
who love us for who we are,
not for what we can do!

Let's pray for people . . .

Please, God,
bless all people who think too badly of themselves:
people who are afraid to do anything
because they're convinced they'll fail.
Please help them to know that they're loved,
and help us to show them that for you.

Jesus on the edge

Based on Matthew 26:36-46

Jesus was very unhappy. He'd just had his last supper with his disciples, and he knew that people who hated him were plotting to get rid of him. He trusted his Father God to work things out, but he knew it was going to be very scary and very painful along the way.

'Let's go out,' he said to his disciples, and they all got up from the table to follow him to the garden of Gethsemane.

'Jesus seems very thoughtful, tonight,' Thomas commented as they went. 'I get the feeling something really dreadful's going to happen.'

'Oh, I wouldn't worry,' James assured him. 'God'll keep us safe – he's good like that – he won't let any harm come to Jesus.'

'Well, I don't know,' Thomas replied. 'I trust God of course, but I don't think it's quite as simple as that.'

By now, they'd got to the garden. They'd never seen Jesus look so upset. 'If I didn't know better, I'd say he was frightened,' said Peter.

Jesus spoke. 'Peter, James and John, you come with me. The rest of you, sit here while I go and pray.'

A little further on, he turned to his three friends and said: 'This is a very difficult time for me. Will you watch with me?' Then he went a little further on his own and lay down on the ground to pray. 'Father, this is awful – isn't there some way I can avoid what's going to happen? Isn't there another way?' Then he took a deep breath, and said: 'But it's your will that matters, so I'll go through it if I have to.'

He got up and walked back to his three friends, who had fallen fast asleep. 'Oh, Peter,' he said, 'couldn't you

A story, a hug and a prayer

manage to stay awake for just one hour, to pray with me? Come on, stay awake – pray that you don't have to go through what I'm going to experience. I know you mean well, but you're just not strong enough to hack it.'

As he went away, the disciples looked at one another. 'What was that all about?' James asked.

'I dunno,' John replied, 'but I wish we could just go home – it's scary here.'

He was right. It was very dark, with the moonlight casting sinister shadows among the trees – but that was nothing compared with the fear that Jesus was feeling as he went away again to pray to his Father. 'It's not that I don't trust you,' he said, 'but this is such a terrible thing I'm going to have to bear, and I really wish there was another way. Surely, we can avoid it somehow? Still, it's your will that matters, not mine.'

When Jesus went back to his friends, they were completely out of it – fast asleep and dead to the world. This time, he didn't wake them but went and prayed again – saying just the same as before. The silence was terrible. Although he prayed harder than he had ever prayed in his life, there seemed to be no answer. Just that awesome silence – not even the rustling of the usual wildlife or the movement of the breeze. Nothing. It was as if all creation was holding its breath to see what Jesus would do.

Jesus knew what he had to do. But knowing didn't make it easy. For what seemed like hours, he lay there on the ground, praying, but all his words seemed just to vanish into the still, horrible silence of the night. Eventually, he got up and went back to his sleeping friends. 'Time to wake up,' he said. 'This is it – I've got to do what God sent me to do. Look, they've come to get me.'

Suddenly, the garden was full of people with swords and sticks, all looking for Jesus. Jesus faced up to them calmly. 'I'm the one you want,' he said. 'Let my friends go.' Peter wanted to make a fight of it, and pulled out a sword, but Jesus stopped him. 'I've preached love and non-violence all my ministry,' he said, 'and I'm not going to throw all that away just to save my own skin.'

Jesus on the edge

So Jesus was captured and led away, and his friends turned and ran.

There was no way back, now. Jesus stayed true to God, and true to his own faith. Even as they nailed him to the cross, he prayed for them and kept on trusting God. When he died, some people thought it was all over – but it wasn't. He'd won the battle – he'd kept faith with God even when everything seemed hopeless. And now, God was going to keep faith with him – soon he would be raised to wonderful new life. That's one of the really great stories Christians have to share – and we'll have it another time.

A story, a hug and a prayer

Let's chat . . .

Sometimes we have to face difficult things,
and there just isn't a way out
– not even one that only God can find.
Sometimes, the only way out is through,
not round the problem.
That's when we really have to trust God!
Let's remember that this story ended
with the happiest happy ending in all history!

We're sad . . .

Wanting to avoid trouble of any kind is natural,
isn't it, God?
And sometimes we try to avoid trouble
by not facing up to things.
Please forgive us, and help us to have real faith.

We're glad . . .

Isn't it great, God,
when we meet really caring people
– the kind who stick with us
through thick and thin?
Thank you for giving us such signs of your love.

Let's pray for people . . .

Please, God, help people in trouble
to know you're with them,
even when they find it hard to see you.
And help us to be the kind of friends
that make you more visible.

Faith raises the roof

Based on Mark 2:1-12

I'm going to tell you about a man with a problem – the Bible doesn't tell us his name, but let's call him Eli. Now, Eli was paralysed. Have you any idea what that meant to him in those days? How d'you think he got around?

People didn't have any of the equipment some disabled people have now – and even now it's not as easy as some able-bodied folk seem to think! Eli had to rely on kind friends to take him everywhere, and probably on his wife to help with things like washing and dressing.

One day, some of Eli's friends heard that Jesus was in the area, and they had enough faith in Jesus to believe that he could heal Eli. So, without more ado, they picked up Eli's mattress between them and carried him to where Jesus was staying. The trouble was, everybody else knew Jesus was around, too – so the place was crowded and they couldn't get in. Some people were standing in the garden, straining to hear what Jesus was saying, and there were even some lying down on the flat roof with their ears pressed against it to try and hear him.

Flat roof! Eli's friends didn't hesitate – which was probably a good thing, because if they'd stopped to think they might never have gone through with their idea. They heaved Eli's mattress – with the terrified Eli clinging to it like a limpet – up the steps at the side of the house and onto the roof. Then they started ripping the lid off the building.

So, there was Jesus, inside the house, teaching the crowd of people – who were all getting a little bit sticky, what with the heat and everything – when suddenly, there was some ventilation. Ben, the owner of the house, wasn't

A story, a hug and a prayer

so happy, though, because the nice fresh air was coming straight through a hole in his roof.

And the next thing to come through the hole was a lot less welcome than the fresh air: a mattress with a man on it, being lowered on ropes.

Now, you'd have thought from his reaction that Jesus saw people coming down from the ceiling every day – he didn't bat an eyelid but just looked at Eli and said: 'Hey, chill out – you're forgiven everything.'

That didn't please some lawyers who were there. 'Only God can forgive sins,' they were thinking. 'So he's just made himself equal with God, and that's against the law.'

Jesus knew what was going on in their heads, and brought it out into the open. 'Look,' he said, 'anyone can *say* sins are forgiven – words are easy – but saying "Get up and walk", well, that's another matter isn't it? I mean, I'd look a bit silly if it didn't happen, wouldn't I? So I'm going to show you that my words have a bit of authority behind them.' Then he turned to Eli – who was still lying on his mattress – and said: 'I'm telling you to get on your feet, pick up that mattress and go home.'

Well, you should have heard the silence! Everybody was holding their breath waiting to see what would happen next. Eli's friends were staring down through the hole they'd made in the roof; Ben was peering back up, wondering who was going to pay for the repairs, and all the people inside the house were waiting to see whether the impossible was going to happen.

Funnily enough, the only person who didn't seem completely paralysed at that moment was Eli – the only person apart from Jesus, that is. He was off his mattress, had it rolled up and tucked under his arm, and before anyone could say 'absolute stupefaction and overwhelming incredulity' he'd walked out of the room and gone home.

Back in the house, the silence didn't last for long. But then, silences never do, which is rather a pity because a good silence is truly golden – but I digress. It started with a single word, almost whispered. And the word was, 'Amazing!'

Faith raises the roof

Then someone else added 'unbelievable', and the ball really started rolling. People started throwing in words like 'extraordinary' and 'miraculous' and in a matter of moments the whole houseful of people were praising God and saying they'd never seen anything like it in their lives.

And Eli? He was just enjoying his new freedom: at last he could look at something more interesting than the sky, without getting a stiff neck!

A story, a hug and a prayer

Let's chat . . .

Wasn't it a good thing
that Eli's friends weren't easily embarrassed!
Maybe there are times we need to 'raise the roof'
on behalf of people who can't stand up for themselves?

We're sad . . .

We're sorry, God,
if we've ever let our friends down
because we were afraid to be pushy!
Help us to know when it's time
to be a nuisance
for the good of someone else.

We're glad . . .

Thank you, God!
Thank you so much for people
who haven't taken no for an answer
where other people's needs have been at stake!
Thank you for people who get things changed
(even if at times we get embarrassed by them!)

Let's pray for people . . .

Please, God, bless all people
who stand up for others who can't.
Give them courage and faith
to keep on trying,
and help us to pay attention.

Moses, Elijah and Jesus

Based on Mark 9:2-10

Now, there are some pretty amazing stories in the Bible – and this is one of them. So, I want you to imagine we're back in the time when Jesus was living his earthly life. Now, see if you can work out where we are. The air's a bit on the cool side for the time of day; we're all a bit out of breath; and there's this incredible view – we can see for miles. So, where do you think we are?

OK, so we're up a mountain. Jesus has come up here with his closest friends, Peter, James and John. And he hasn't told them why. Perhaps we can hear them talking.

'I don't know what this is all about,' Peter's saying, 'but it'd better be good. I'm a seaman, I am – not a mountain man.'

James and John have probably got their own theories. We know James and John were a bit full of themselves – wanted to be the top people, and thought Jesus was going to give them power. We can just hear John saying: 'He's brought us up here to look at our kingdom, that's what. One day, we'll be in charge of all this – isn't that right, James?'

'You – in charge?' Peter scoffs. 'Jesus wouldn't put you two in charge of a compost heap – he's got more sense!'

Just a minute, though – what's happening? Jesus is starting to look really odd – his robe is starting to glow. And as we watch, it gets brighter and brighter, until it's almost too dazzling to look at!

'All right,' we can hear James saying to the others. 'If you're so all-fired clever, explain that.'

No one can, of course – but it's about to get even more weird. Suddenly there are two other men there, talking

A story, a hug and a prayer

with Jesus. Not ordinary men – to be honest, they look a bit wild: they've got long beards, untidy hair, and clothes that most people certainly wouldn't wear to church, let alone to meet Jesus face to face – well, not without giving them a good ironing, anyway.

'It's Moses and Elijah!' James whispers.

'Of course it is,' says John. 'Anybody can see that.'

Now why it's so obvious isn't really – um – obvious, but they all seem agreed about it. The people talking with Jesus are Moses and Elijah. Now, Peter's always been one to get carried away – so you can imagine how he reacts. 'Hey, Teacher!' he says. 'Is this terrific, or is this terrific! Why don't we make three shelters here – one for you, one for Moses and one for Elijah? Then we could just stay here, all the time, couldn't we?'

The truth is, poor old Peter's really as scared as everyone else and doesn't honestly know what to say. So instead of saying nothing, he's saying anything – anything that comes into his head – without thinking about it first. Peter's trouble is he's got a mouth like a tumble dryer – he opens his mouth and whatever thought happens to be at the front falls out!

Anyway, back to the story. There they are, all pretty frightened and trying not to show it, when the whole scene gets even more spooky. I mean, on a clear day, when you can see for miles, suddenly there's this thick, black cloud. No rain – just a cloud, coming from nowhere – and it covers everybody. And then there's a voice – seems to come from the cloud itself. 'This is my Son,' it booms. 'This is the special one – pay attention to him.'

So, we've got Jesus, with his robes shining and glittering like disco lighting; we've got these two old guys – Moses and Elijah, who we all know have been dead for centuries; we've got a big, dark cloud; and we've got a voice coming from nowhere. What d'you make of all that, then?

Too late! It's gone! There's Peter with his face buried in the grass, pretending to be looking for grasshoppers but shaking and trembling as if he's just found out he can do

Moses, Elijah and Jesus

it, and James and John gazing around them with their mouths open – and Jesus, standing there all alone as though nothing's happened at all.

'Time to go,' he says. 'We can't stay up here all the time – there's work to do.'

So, they start off down the mountain again, with James and John all agog to find out what it all meant.

'Come on, Jesus – what was all that about?' James asks him.

"That's not for you to know at the moment,' Jesus says, mysteriously. 'And don't go blabbing about this to everyone else, either – got it? You can tell them all about it after I've risen from the dead.'

'Risen from the dead?' says Peter. 'Now, there's an idea – but what does it mean?' And so they walk away, down the mountain again – gassing away among themselves, and leaving us to work out what it was all about.

A story, a hug and a prayer

Let's chat . . .

> *Isn't it great?*
> *Occasionally, God gives us little glimpses of glory:*
> *a kindness from the last person we'd expect,*
> *or a really creative idea by someone we thought*
> *was 'just ordinary'!**

We're sad . . .

> *Please forgive us, Lord,*
> *for stopping looking when we think we've seen.*
> *Help us to look more deeply at life.*
> *Help us to see your greater value and purpose*
> *behind the 'ordinary' things.*

We're glad . . .

> *Thank you, Lord, for all that's not obvious!*
> *Thank you for the things we only find*
> *when we climb mountains, or dig deep,*
> *or look or listen more carefully.*
> *Thank you for a wonderful, multi-layered creation!*

Let's pray for people . . .

> *Please, God, give all people*
> *the insight to see your glory in the world.*

---

* And remember: there's nothing wrong with being 'ordinary' – more things are achieved by 'ordinary' people than by 'extraordinary' ones.

It's a power thing

Based on Mark 10:35-45

Jesus knew the next few moments were going to be difficult. He couldn't hear what James and John were saying, but they were huddled together deep in conversation. And that always meant they were plotting something.

'It's no good putting it off,' John hissed to his brother. 'Jesus is going to be a real big-shot one day, and the way things are going Peter's going to be right up there with him, where *we* should be.'

'Peter?' James echoed, incredulously. 'Peter? Whatever makes you think Jesus would choose Peter? The man's a loser – all mouth and no stomach for action.'

'You know that, and I know that,' John answered, patiently. 'But you know Jesus – always sees the best in people. If we don't get it sorted out now, it'll be too late.'

So they went over to see Jesus. Although he was expecting trouble, Jesus listened to them carefully – just the way he always did.

'Excuse me, Jesus,' John began, 'but there's something we'd like you to do for us.'

'Oh, dear!' thought Jesus. 'I knew it! Why do so many people only talk to me when they want something? Why can't they just come and natter about normal things like weather, and how the children are doing at school?' He turned to James and John. 'OK, spit it out.'

John nudged his brother. 'Go on, James, tell him.'

'Me?' James was indignant. 'It was your idea – *you* tell him.'

John blushed. 'It wasn't my idea, at all.'

'Oh, yes it was.'

'Oh, no, it wasn't.'

A story, a hug and a prayer

Now, Jesus was a patient person, but this was testing even him.

'Just cut the buck-passing,' he said, 'and get on with it.'

John nudged James so hard that James stumbled forward and John quickly stepped behind him. 'Go on, James, I'm right behind you, all the way.'

James took a deep breath. 'Well, Jesus, it's like this. We thought – well, our mother thought – yes, that's it – our mother thought we ought to ask you . . .'

Jesus fixed a piercing look on him. 'Ask me what?'

'Well, you know when you come into your kingdom – you know, when God makes you the big shot over everybody? Well, we just wondered where we were going to stand.'

'Sit.' John corrected him. 'We wondered where we were going to sit.'

'That's right,' James added. 'We thought that one on each side of you would be nice – you know, sort of close to the seat of power, that sort of thing.'

'Right, so it's power you want, is it?' Jesus replied. 'Well, what about all the other stuff? Can you share the pain I'm going to have to suffer? Can you be part of *everything* that's going to happen to me?'

'Oh, we can, we can,' they chorused together.

'And you will,' Jesus assured them. 'But when it comes to sitting near my throne, and sharing the glory, well, that's not for me to say. That's for my Father God to decide.'

Just then, a voice cut in. 'Just who do you two think you are?' James and John turned to find a very angry Simon Peter standing behind them, and around him a group of other disciples – and they didn't look as though they'd come to say 'God bless'!

'Let's get this straight,' Jesus said. 'In the rest of the world, kings and rulers may be all high and mighty, but not with you. Any of you – *any* of you – who wants to be great is going to have to serve everybody. After all, that's what I've come to do.'

James and John looked at the angry faces around them. 'Um, yes, of course, Jesus,' James faltered. 'Serve everybody.

It's a power thing

Absolutely right. That's it, then – when it comes to being a servant I'll be the greatest.'

'No you won't,' John objected. '*I* will!'

'Oh no, you won't!'

'Oh yes, I will!'

'Oh no . . .'

I think we'd better just leave it there. Don't you?

A story, a hug and a prayer

Let's chat . . .

It's not unnatural to want to be important;
most of us do.
The secret is of course, that we all are:
important to God and each other.
What causes the trouble
is our wanting to be more *important than others.*

We're sad . . .

We all want to do well in life.
There's nothing wrong with that, is there, God?
Sometimes, though, that's just not enough
and we start wanting to control others
for our own benefit.
Please forgive us.

We're glad . . .

We want to say 'thank you', God,
for people who care;
people who find their own importance
in helping others.
Those people change the world for us all!
Thank you!

Let's pray for people . . .

We pray for all people
who think they aren't important,
and that others don't respect them enough.
Please give them confidence in their own value,
and help them find that in valuing others.

The boy Jesus in the temple

Luke 2:41-52

Mary was half-walking, half-dancing along the road. 'Wasn't the festival wonderful?' she kept saying. 'I could have danced for ever!'

'Looks to me like you're going to!' Joseph replied. 'I don't know where you get all the energy.'

'It was terrific,' Mary continued – as if she hadn't heard Joseph at all. 'The food, the music, the dancing – where *did* that drummer get all his ideas from? Jesus loved it, didn't he!'

Joseph looked around anxiously and said, 'Talking of Jesus – where *has* that boy got to? I really wish he wouldn't just wander off.'

'I expect he's with his cousins,' Mary answered. 'I mean, what 12-year-old boy wants to walk with his parents! Or maybe he's made some new friends among the other pilgrims.'

Joseph went off to check, and came back looking worried. 'I can't find him,' he said. 'I've looked everywhere – the only place he can be is back in Jerusalem.'

Mary's feet weren't dancing any more as they left the group and walked back to the city. They were striding purposefully on, and the smile on her face had turned to a half-worried, half-angry frown.

When they got back to the city, it was hard to know where to look first – it was still teeming with people, many of them carrying big packs, or leading donkeys loaded with luggage.

'Jesus could be anywhere,' Mary said, anxiously. 'You remember how he was into everything while we were here.'

A story, a hug and a prayer

'Well, let's start with the fairs,' said Joseph. 'Some of those entertainers really got him interested – I won't be surprised if he'd persuaded them to give him an extra show!'

Several hours – and four aching feet – later, Mary had to admit it. 'We've got nowhere at all!' she said.

'Try telling that to my feet!' Joseph countered. 'We may have got nowhere, but we've *been* everywhere!'

'Well, we can't just stop,' Mary said. 'We've got to keep on and on looking.'

So they did – for three solid days. Can you imagine it? Three days without sleeping, with only quick snacks to keep them going – they were frantic with worry, and that just kept driving them on and on. And all the time, at the back of their minds was the terrible thought: if Jesus hadn't hung back to watch the last of the entertainment, then what *could* have happened?

'He's made a lot of new friends,' Joseph said. 'Perhaps he went to say goodbye to them.'

'That's no help at all, is it?' Mary objected. 'Most of them were from other pilgrim groups, and they've started for home. If he's got in with them, he could be anywhere in Israel by now!'

'We'd better go to the temple,' Joseph said. 'We'll have to report this to the authorities.'

So they made their way to the temple, and looked for one of the officials. 'Look,' Joseph pointed. 'There's a crowd of people over there – must be something going on, so we'll find someone we can talk to.'

As they got closer, they realised there was a debate in progress. It was a really deep conversation about God, the world, what life really means, and all that kind of stuff. Joseph didn't want to interrupt at first, but as they got closer he stopped in amazement.

'Hey, Mary!' he said. 'Am I dreaming, or what?'

'Well, if it's a dream I'm having it, too!' Mary answered. Then she raised her voice. 'Jesus! What on earth d'you think you're doing? D'you think these important people

The boy Jesus in the temple

haven't got better things to do than gossip with you? And have you any idea how worried we've been?'

Jesus looked at her, calmly. 'Worried? Why on earth should you be worried,' he asked. 'Didn't you know that I'd be in my Father's house and about his business?'

Well, that went right over their heads: they didn't have a clue what he was talking about, and anyway all they really wanted to do was get him home to Nazareth. Mary never forgot what he'd said, though. Something told her it wasn't just childish nonsense.

And she was right.

A story, a hug and a prayer

Let's chat . . .

Questions are OK!
They're not always convenient,
or easy to answer.
They may be impossible *to answer!*
But that doesn't mean we shouldn't ask!

We're sad . . .

Sometimes, God, we shy away
from the difficult questions.
Probably, we're afraid of where the answers may lead us.
Help us to trust you, even when the answers seem hard.

We're glad . . .

What a wonderful world!
There's so much we don't understand!
So much for us to ask and learn about!
Thank you, God, for the unanswered questions!

Let's pray for people . . .

You know, God,
it must be really hard for people
who are afraid to ask;
who want to question things
but have been told they shouldn't!
Please help us all to be more curious!

Jesus challenges us with love

Based on Luke 4:16-30

Can you imagine a full-scale riot breaking out during a service because of something the preacher said? Well, Jesus started one at his synagogue in Nazareth.

Imagine the scene: the place is full of people – nearly everybody in the town goes to worship – and one of them is Jesus. He's just come back from taking some time out to listen to God, so they're probably pleased to see him – and then someone asks him to read the Bible reading.

'It's from the book of Isaiah,' Jesus announces. 'This is what the prophet Isaiah says: "God's chosen me, and given me his Spirit – he's put his power into me. I've to go and tell his good news. Not just any old good news – good news specially for all the poor people. Oh, yes – I'm here to set all captives free. I'm here to make blind people see again, and everyone who's being bullied by people in power – well, they're going to be free of that. This is it, folks – this is the time of God's choosing when he's going to change things in this here world." '

Now, everyone's paying attention. They've all completely forgotten the gossip they'd been going to share – and no one's even bothering to look for who's wearing the nicest clothes. Suddenly, they've got the idea that this morning might be interesting. So they're all just waiting there, quietly. And every single eye is looking straight at Jesus. 'Right now,' he says, 'this prophecy has come true, right here where you are!'

Just in front of you, you can see old Rachel, the flower steward, lean across to her husband. 'Ooh,' she says, 'Don't he talk lovely! Don't you think so, Ben?'

101

A story, a hug and a prayer

Ben doesn't look so happy, though. 'Who does he think he is?' he grumbles. 'His dad's the local carpenter – what does he know about prophecy?'

Jesus hasn't finished yet, though. 'I know what you're all thinking!' he says. 'You're wondering why I don't do miracles here, like the ones you've heard I've done elsewhere.'

'Well?' Ben calls out, 'Why don't you?'

'I'll tell you,' Jesus answers. 'Because prophets can't work in their home towns – people won't accept them.'

'What d'you know about it?' Ben objects. 'You're just a local boy!'

Jesus is really getting going, now. His eyes are shining, and his face is full of colour as he looks straight at Ben. 'Look in your Bible,' he says, 'and ask yourself: why did Elijah have to go and help a foreign widow – weren't there enough widows in Israel? And what about Naaman – weren't there people in Israel who needed healing at that time? So why did Elisha only heal a foreigner?'

Old Rachel turns to her husband again. 'He's got a point, ain't he?' she says. 'Prophets always get driven away, don't they.'

'Load of rubbish!' Ben objects. 'If he goes on talking like that he's going to get thrown out of here.'

Mind you, you can hardly hear what they're saying because the whole congregation's shouting insults at Jesus and telling him to go away – but I won't tell you what they're actually saying, because they aren't as polite as I am.

Then, suddenly, everyone's on their feet all around us. The noise is amazing – people shouting and stamping their feet – and it feels like United have lost at home and we're in the wrong enclosure. *Well* scary! Even old Rachel has got caught up in it. 'Get him!' she's shouting. 'Throw him out! Go on, parson – give him a bunch of fives.'

Suddenly, Ben's at it, too. 'Take him to the cliff!' he's shouting.

Well, I won't tell you all the details – it's not very nice seeing religious people behave like that – but right at the last minute, right at the cliff edge, Jesus sort of fixes the

Jesus challenges us with love

mob with his eyes, and he seems to pull them up short. You can almost hear them thinking, 'What are we doing? How did we get from worshipping God to trying to kill the preacher?'

Jesus begins to walk forward, and as he does so the crowd fall back and let him through. But it just goes to show – it's not just the people out there who need prophets to remind them to love each other. It's us, too.

A story, a hug and a prayer

Let's chat . . .

> *People we know aren't 'special', are they?*
> *How can they be – they seem so ordinary!*
> *Sometimes, we're so busy peering into the distance*
> *that we miss what's under our nose!*

We're sad . . .

> *I sometimes think, Lord,*
> *that we should value 'ordinary' people more.*
> *You know – the ones we bump into*
> *in our daily lives.*
> *Forgive us for always looking elsewhere*
> *for 'special' people.*

We're glad . . .

> *Thank, you, God,*
> *for what's 'special' in each of us.*
> *Thank you for making 'ordinary' people*
> *with 'extraordinary' qualities!*
> *Please help us appreciate one another more.*

Let's pray for people . . .

> *We want to pray for each other, God:*
> *for the people who are really special to us,*
> *and who also happen to be very close to us!*
> *Help us to know how important we are*
> *to one another.*

Lots of love

Based on Luke 7:37-50

Now, it wasn't that Jo wanted to make herself the centre of attention. Jo was used to being kept at arm's length until she was wanted. And even then, people would probably sneak round to see her when they thought nobody was looking. Jo wasn't the kind of person that respectable people wanted to be seen talking to.

Folk would even cross the street to avoid getting too close to Jo; they had this strange idea that sinfulness was catching – you know, like yawning: once one person does it, everyone wants to.

'Come, now, Benjamin,' she heard someone say. 'We don't want to get contaminated, do we? – not when we're having lunch with Jesus at Simon's place.'

'No, Judith dear, of course not.' Benjamin dutifully followed Judith across the road, far away from Jo.

That was the last straw. 'I hate living like this!' Jo thought. 'No friends, no self-respect – I'm going to change, and I know just the man to help me do it. So, Jesus is at Simon's place, is he?'

Simon's place was posh – really upmarket, you know what I mean? You didn't go to Simon's place unless you'd washed at least twice behind your ears and made sure you'd got a clean hanky. And if you'd got Jo's reputation, you still didn't go. But Jo was determined.

'Now, I really should take him a present,' she thought. The only thing Jo had that was valuable was a jar of perfume – the real stuff, it was, classy, and in a jar made of real alabaster. 'I'll take him that,' she thought, 'the most precious thing I've got.'

A story, a hug and a prayer

As she got nearer, Jo started to feel more and more nervous – in fact 'blind panic' might be a good way of putting it. 'Who do I think I am,' she asked herself, 'just turning up to see someone like Jesus?' She arrived at Simon's house, and crept nervously in. She heard Simon's voice.

'Of course, Jesus,' he was saying, 'only the best people come to my dinner parties – we don't allow just any old riff-raff in here.'

Jo knew it was now or never – she had to get in there before her nerve failed. She pushed the door open. Well! She'd never seen so many posh frocks and fancy hats in one place in her life – and the *women's* clothes were even better.

'Who on earth let that woman in here?' Simon bellowed. 'Stop her someone!'

Jo ran like she'd never run before – straight toward Jesus. She'd completely lost it, by now, and tears were just pouring down her face – and she hadn't really worked out what it was she was going to say or do, but she fell down right by Jesus' feet. She could tell he'd had a long journey and hadn't had a chance to wash them – so she broke open the jar and let that wonderful perfume flow all over those sweaty, dusty feet!

Simon turned to the person next to him. 'Just look at Jesus,' he murmured. 'You'd think this was just an everyday event. Of course – if he was what he's cracked up to be, he'd know what kind of woman she is and wouldn't let her near him.'

Jo was in a right old state – crying so much that Jesus' feet were soaked, and she was trying to wipe them dry with her own hair. Jesus turned to Simon. 'Simon, I've got a question to ask you.'

'Oh,' Simon said, 'a privilege indeed – the great teacher wants to ask me a question. Well?'

'There's this moneylender, see,' Jesus said, 'and two people owe him money – one owes thousands of pounds, and the other just a few pennies, but they can't pay – so he just writes off the debts. Now, which of them's going to love him more?'

Lots of love

'Easy peasy!' Simon crowed. 'The one who owed the most in the first place – obvious, isn't it?'

'Fine,' Jesus answered. 'Well, I'm your guest and you haven't given me any kind of welcome – not even the traditional water to wash my feet. She's used her own tears for that, and her hair as a towel. I didn't get a kiss of friendship from you, but she's been kissing my feet continually. And as for anointing me with oil, which any self-respecting Jewish host would do, you just couldn't be bothered – but don't worry, she's done it for you with that beautiful perfume. You see, she's got a lot to be forgiven for, so she knows what love means. Someone who thinks they don't need forgiveness – mentioning no names, of course – well, they just wouldn't be able to show that kind of love. Would they?'

Then Jesus turned to Jo. 'The past is over,' he said. 'You're forgiven.'

Judith, along with the rest of the guests, was horrified. 'Well, I never!' she exclaimed.

'Neither did I, dear!' replied Benjamin.

'Who does he think he is to forgive people,' Judith continued, 'God or someone?'

'You're absolutely right, dear,' Benjamin agreed. 'Shouldn't be allowed.'

Jesus just carried on talking to Jo: 'Your faith's saved you, so go in peace.'

A story, a hug and a prayer

Let's chat . . .

*Isn't it interesting how we label people
without really knowing them.
'Typical man!'
'Just like a woman!'
'Anyone who dresses like that . . .'
I'm glad Jesus doesn't do that!*

We're sad . . .

*Sorry, God – we've been and done it again!
We see people, and we judge them –
it happens far too often.
Forgive us for being too quick
to jump to conclusions about people.*

We're glad . . .

*Just sometimes, God, we meet really special people:
people who seem to see the good in us
even when we're having a bad prayer day!
Thank you for them!*

Let's pray for people . . .

*Please, God,
bless all people who get shoved aside,
because of other people's prejudices.
Teach us all to be more open to others,
and help us to be a sign of your love
to all who are treated like dirt.*

Love is a seed to be sown

Based on Luke 8:4-8

Jesus wanted to show how God loves us so much that he just scatters his love around everywhere – even in places where it seems hopeless. So he told a story a bit like this one.

Mike was a farmer and he was getting a hard time from Joe, his accountant, who thought he was a little bit reckless. 'You don't mean you sow *all* your seed in the ground?' he gasped in amazement. 'Don't you keep some in reserve, just in case?'

'Every single seed' Mike assured him. 'And I get a good harvest every year.'

'Well, that's all very well,' said his accountant, 'but I hope you're careful where you scatter it.'

Mike's wife, Sally, thought that was hilarious. 'Careful? Him?' she laughed. 'You really ought to watch him sowing – it'd be an education for you.'

So it was that, when the sowing season came round again, Joe was there to watch Mike at work. At first, he thought Mike must have gone stark, staring mad. Mike came leaping out of the house, with a bag of seed over his shoulder, and started laughing and frolicking around like a child at play, instead of a serious businessman at his work!

'Isn't it a wonderful day!' shouted Mike as he pirouetted across the field. 'What a good time to scatter seed! What a great time to dance through the ploughed fields. What a *wonderful* time to wave your arms about and shout for joy!'

Joe was horrified! 'Hey!' he yelled, 'mind the path – how d'you expect anything to grow there?'

A story, a hug and a prayer

Mike just turned a cartwheel and danced on, and as soon as he was a safe distance away, the birds came for a free dinner. 'Well, that's a waste, for a start!' Joe exclaimed.

'Oh, I don't know,' said Sally, 'you're glad enough to have the birds around when they're eating the slugs and snails, so look on it as an investment.'

'Women!' Joe scoffed. Then he yelled, 'Look out, Mike – there's no point in sowing seeds among all those rocks – nothing can grow there!'

The thing that really irritated Joe was that Mike didn't appear to mind if some of his seed was wasted. He didn't seem at all concerned when seeds landed in the briar patch, among all the thistles and nettles – he just went on dancing around and scattering the seed as if it were some sort of a game.

'What you're watching,' said Sally, with a smile, 'is a creative genius who loves his work!'

'What I'm watching,' Joe corrected her, 'is an irresponsible juvenile wasting valuable resources. I'm not at all sure I can continue to manage his affairs if he's going to behave like that.'

'Well,' Sally responded, 'he's been behaving like that ever since I've known him, and you've never complained about the results.'

Joe wasn't listening – he was watching in amazement as Mike stood up to his knees in a waterlogged part of the field and thrust both hands into his seed bag. Laughing merrily, he threw his arms wide and a shower of seed erupted all around him. Some landed in the puddles, some got into his hair or fell into his pockets – and quite a lot got carried away by the wind.

Mike was all smiles as he trudged back across the field. 'I love this job,' he said. 'All this seed, all this possibility – and I can just scatter it everywhere! Scatter, scatter, scatter!' And he laughed with sheer joy.

'Humph!' Joe snorted. 'You'll be bankrupt in a year, just wait and see.'

Mike and Sally waited. And they saw. They saw the birds continue eating the seed on the paths; they noticed the

Love is a seed to be sown

seed that had landed on the rocks, growing and then dying for lack of water; they watched as the wheat that sprung up in the briars got choked and died. And they watched as, all over the field, little green shoots appeared, grew, and turned into wonderful golden corn, waving joyfully at the sun.

After the harvest, they invited Joe back to check the accounts. 'I can't understand it,' Joe groaned. 'You just scattered that seed in that stupid, irresponsible way, and it's gone and produced a hundred times as much. What is it – some sort of magic?'

Mike and Sally roared with laughter. 'That isn't magic, Joe,' Sally told him. 'That's love!'

A story, a hug and a prayer

Let's chat . . .

Ever thought of God as irresponsible?
Generous, maybe, but surely not irresponsible?
No? Good!
Scattering love around even where it seems wasted;
that's not irresponsible – it's divine.
And sometimes, the unexpected happens.

We're sad . . .

It's a tough call, you know, God,
being asked to love like that.
We can't do it, of course,
but perhaps we could get a little closer than we do!

We're glad . . .

You can do it, though, can't you!
You love like that all the time
– and often it hurts you.
Thank you, God, for all your love.

Let's pray for people . . .

We're thinking about people
who just can't believe in that kind of love;
people who think they have to be good to be loved,
and blame themselves for not being good enough.
Help them to know that you love them
just as they are.

Taking the time to care

Based on Luke 8:42b-48

Chloe could see that Jesus was a man in a hurry. He'd just been asked to go and save a 12-year-old girl who was dying. The girl's father was a local religious leader, and Chloe knew that he was very important. Now, Chloe had come here specially to see Jesus. She'd been ill for years – it was a very not-nice illness, and no one could cure her – and she was hoping Jesus would help, but now he was rushing away.

One of Jesus' friends, Peter, was trying to clear the way for him – just like Peter, always wanting to be in charge of things. 'Clear the way,' he was shouting, 'clear the way. Jesus is on an urgent life-saving mission. Clear the way.'

Chloe could understand how Peter felt – no one had seen such a crowd since the Jerusalem Rangers played the Samaritan Stags for the league cup. 'Oh, I mustn't trouble Jesus,' she thought, 'I'm not important enough for that, and he's much too busy. But if I can just touch his coat I'm sure I'll get better.'

Soon, Jesus drew level with Chloe. She let him go past before she reached out and touched his coat.

Jesus stopped. 'Who touched me?' he asked.

Everyone suddenly started feeling guilty for some strange reason. 'It wasn't me,' said one.

'Not me, either,' said another.

'My hands are in my pockets, so it couldn't have been me, could it?' protested a third.

'Well, someone did,' Jesus said very firmly, 'and I'd really like to know who.'

Peter interrupted. 'Oh, get real, Jesus,' he said. 'There are crowds all round you, pressing in against you, and

A story, a hug and a prayer

you're asking who touched you? Most of them could hardly avoid it, I should think.'

'I didn't say, "jostled", Jesus corrected him. 'I said, "touched". Someone reached out and touched me, and some power went out of me. I just want to know who it was, that's all.'

Chloe was feeling terribly guilty, now. All this time Jesus could be on his way to that important man's little girl, and he was wasting it on her! 'I'd better own up,' she thought. 'Then he can get on his way.'

Chloe took a deep breath and stepped forward. 'I'm sorry,' she said to Jesus, 'but it was me. I didn't mean any harm – honestly – I really hope you're not angry – I just wanted to get better – 12 years I'd had that illness, and touching your coat has cured it – I didn't mean any harm, and I'm truly, truly sorry. Truly.'

Then Chloe saw that Jesus was smiling – he didn't look angry, at all. Other people didn't seem so happy, though. The man who had asked Jesus for help was looking really frantic – and Chloe could understand why. 'After all,' she thought, 'his little girl's dying – I was only ill.'

Peter leaned forward and tried to urge Jesus on. 'Whatever it is, it's over,' he said. 'Why hang around here when there's urgent business to do?'

'Don't worry, I'll deal with that later,' Jesus assured him calmly. 'Right now, this woman needs me, and I want to give time to her.'

Chloe could hardly believe her ears. 'Me – he wants to give time to me!' she thought. 'No one's ever said that before – especially someone in a hurry.'

Jesus took her hand. 'It's your faith that's healed you,' Jesus told her. 'Now go, and be happy.'

Chloe was over the moon! 'My illness has gone – he could have left it at that,' she thought, 'but he seemed to know that I really needed that little bit extra. He found time for me, even though he was in a hurry.' So all the way home Chloe said to herself over and over again, 'I'm well – and I'm important. I'm well – and I'm important.' Some-

Taking the time to care

thing told her that her life was never going to be the same again, now that she'd met Jesus.

Oh, and in case you're wondering, Jesus saved the little girl, too – even though everyone thought he was too late. But that's another story.

A story, a hug and a prayer

Let's chat . . .

Panic, rush, stress, overload!
Isn't life often like that?
It takes a really special person to stay calm in a crisis
and get the priorities right.

We're sad . . .

Something tells us, God,
that an awful lot of people get left out,
because we're all too frantic to notice them.
Please forgive us, and make us more aware.

We're glad . . .

You know, God, it's well impressive
how some folk always have time.
It's not that they're lazy,
they just always seem to have time for others.
Thank you for people like that.

Let's pray for people . . .

It must be horrible to be left out, Lord,
always to be the one no one notices,
or has time for.
Help us to be like Jesus for them,
always to notice – and to have time.

God's basic law of love

Based on Luke 10:25-37

Have you noticed how some people get a real hang-up about rules? Now, don't get me wrong: we all need rules to help us live properly – it's just that some folk think they're the answer to absolutely everything. And that's how Jesus came to tell this story – well, one very like it, anyway. A man asked him: 'What do I have to do to get to heaven?'

Jesus knew what the guy was up to – he was trying to catch Jesus out. So Jesus just said, 'What does the law say? What d'you read in your Bible?'

'Easy!' the man answered. 'Love God – like, really love him – and love your neighbour the way you love yourself.'

'Fine,' said Jesus. 'Do that and you'll not go wrong.'

The man wasn't satisfied with that, though, was he! 'Yeah, yeah, yeah,' he said, 'but what do you mean by "neighbour"?' Well, he asked for it! Jesus answered by telling a story, a lot like this one:

Imagine someone walking from Jerusalem to Jericho. Jesus didn't tell us his name, but we'll call him Bart, for now. So, Bart decides he wants to go to Jericho. He really ought to know better, because the Jericho road's well dangerous – not because of the traffic, but bandits. The hills around it are crawling with them, and they'll rob anything that moves! Still, Bart's not worried by that – he thinks he can take care of himself. So, off he goes – and it's not long before he's lying at the side of the road, covered in blood, and thinking he's going to die.

Then he hears footsteps. 'Thank you, God!' he says. 'Someone's going to help me.' Very painfully, he turns his head to look down the road, and sees a priest coming along.

A story, a hug and a prayer

The priest doesn't even come near to him – just crosses right over to the other side of the road and keeps going. 'Sorry,' he calls out, 'can't touch blood at the moment – I've got a service to take, and worshipping with blood on my hands would be against all the rules. Sorry, and all that.' And to Bart's utter amazement, he scuttles past and leaves him there.

Next guy along is a Levite – another kind of religious leader – and Bart really thinks he's going to help, but exactly the same thing happens. 'I'm ever so sorry,' the Levite calls as he passes, 'but you might be dead, for all I know – and if I touch a dead body it'll take me weeks to get clean again. Sorry, but it's the rules.' And off he goes, on the other side of the road.

Well – what's poor old Bart to do? He can't move because of the blood loss and sunstroke, and he really thinks he's going to die. So, when he hears more footsteps coming, he doesn't really hope for very much at all – especially when he sees that it's a Samaritan. Now, what you need to know is that Samaritans and Jews don't talk to each other. In fact, they hate one another. Jews think Samaritans have got their religion all wrong, and Samaritans think Jews are stuck-up snobs – and that *they've* got *their* religion wrong!

'Well, this is no good,' Bart thinks, 'no good at all. Here I am, lying here with blood leaking out everywhere and the people I thought would help me didn't – I've got no chance with a lousy, rotten Samaritan.' But then an incredible thing happens. The Samaritan – let's call him Joe, to save time – he goes over to where Bart's lying, and looks down at him.

'Good grief!' Joe exclaims. 'You've really been in the wars, haven't you! I'll soon get you somewhere safe.' Then he kneels down on the road and gives Bart first aid – cleans up his wounds, bandages them, and then says: 'Let's get you onto my donkey – there's an inn just down the road where you can be looked after.'

So, next thing Bart knows is that he's in a nice clean bed

God's basic law of love

in a fancy inn, being cared for by the innkeeper – and Joe, the 'lousy, rotten Samaritan', is handing over his own money to pay for it! 'Just make sure he's looked after,' Joe says, 'and next time I'm here I'll pay you whatever else I owe.'

So, that's the story Jesus told. Then he turned to the man who'd asked the question, and said, 'So, who do *you* think was a neighbour to the injured man?'

'That's easy!' the man answered. 'The one who helped him.'

'Great!' Jesus answered. 'So why don't you just stop trying to catch me out and go and do the same?'

That wasn't what the man had wanted to hear. He'd always thought keeping the rules was simple – but he'd reckoned without God's basic rule of love. And he'd never imagined it would mean he had to be nice to Samaritans!

A story, a hug and a prayer

Let's chat . . .

> Sometimes the good people
> are the last ones we'd consider.
> What kinds of prejudices do we come across?

We're sad . . .

> We all do it, God,
> at least occasionally.
> We see someone dressed a certain way,
> or living in a certain area,
> and we just assume they're bad – or snobbish.
> Please forgive us for being prejudiced.

We're glad . . .

> Sometimes, people challenge us, don't they?
> They do unexpectedly good things,
> or make surprisingly intelligent conversation.
> Thank you, God, for good and interesting people
> who give us wonderful surprises.

Let's pray for people . . .

> Some people never get the chances they should have
> because other people are prejudiced.
> Please, God, help us to show your love
> to the 'neighbours' whom others don't recognise.

For love or money

Based on Luke 12:16-21

Ike was having a wonderful time. He'd got the builders in – and we're not talking minor house extensions here, either. The builders were building barns, for Ike's farm – the biggest barns you'd ever be likely to see. 'Get your backs into it!' Ike shouted at the workmen. 'I'll need all these barns ready in time for harvest. It's been a really good year, you know.' And he strutted away, rubbing his hands and beaming to himself as he thought how rich he was gong to become.

'I'll never need to work again,' he thought. 'This year's harvest will set me up for life.'

As he walked away, he met Eli, the local priest, coming to see him. 'I'm glad I've found you,' said Eli.

'Whatever you want, the answer's no,' grunted Ike. 'I haven't got time or money to waste on other people.'

'But you could spare a bit of land,' Eli insisted. 'That's all we need – just to make a little playground for the children to use. Wouldn't it be nice for you to have children playing nearby?'

'Look,' said Ike, 'why not come and see me again next year? It's not that I don't want to help, but I need to know I'm OK first. When I've made sure I've got no worries about myself, then I'll help you. But right now, I'm busy providing for my future.'

As Eli walked sadly away, Ike went home. 'I'd like to help,' he thought, 'but I just need to be sure I'll be all right. When I retire, with lots of time and money, then I'll be able to help others.'

Now, what Ike didn't know was that there wasn't going to be any future. If he'd known that, he might have acted

A story, a hug and a prayer

differently – but of course, however rich you are, there are some things you just can't plan for.

Ike went home and made himself a bedtime drink. Children, playing near his fields. Yes, that would be nice. Ike had been lonely all his life – well, when you're determined to make money, things like friends and family have to wait until later. 'Perhaps when the barns are built,' he thought, 'and all my crops are stored away, and I'm sure of a comfortable retirement – then I'll start making some friends. I'll have time for it, then.'

There was a knock on the door. It was Joanna, the woman who lived just down the road from Ike's farm. 'Hello,' she said, 'I'm sorry to bother you, but we're collecting for old Amos. You know he hasn't been well for a while, and now he needs some special treatment that costs a lot of money. Well, he's such a lovely old chap, isn't he, and everyone's given me something. Could you spare a couple of coins?'

Ike really wished this had happened later. In a couple of weeks he'd know the crops were safe, and he could give something then. But this was just too soon for him to take risks. 'I'm sorry,' he said, 'I'm saving for my retirement. Come back in a couple of weeks, and I'll know whether I can afford to give or not.'

Joanna looked shocked. 'If he doesn't get his treatment, Amos won't be here in a couple of weeks,' she said. 'Anyway, you must be able to afford something for a man like him – he's so well loved.'

Ike was getting angry – but only because he was feeling guilty. 'If he's so well loved,' he shouted, 'then I've no doubt you'll get enough from other people. I have to take care of myself, because I haven't got people who love me.'

'No, and I'm not surprised!' replied Joanna, angrily. 'I hope you have a long, lonely retirement, Ike.'

Well, the most amazing thing happened, that night. Ike died. Just like that. No one knew why – perhaps he had a strange disease that didn't have any symptoms. Anyway, whatever it was, he died. All alone. No one to hold his

For love or money

hand, or comfort him. And when the news got out, nobody cried.

Eli the priest did Ike's funeral, and he didn't expect any mourners to be there, because Ike had no friends. But there was just one. Old Amos struggled along to pay his respects. 'Poor Ike,' he said. 'I always felt sorry for him, all alone in that big house. And I'm so well off, with all the friends I've got.'

Poor Ike! All that wealth, and no one to love!

A story, a hug and a prayer

Let's chat . . .

We get our values well twisted at times, don't we?
Let's take time to appreciate each other. Every single day!

We're sad . . .

We've done it again, God!
It's so easy, isn't it?
We get hung up on things
and forget that it's people that matter.
Please help us to keep our values straight.

We're glad . . .

It's the sheer kindness that gets to us, God!
Some people just seem so content with so little
and have so much to give to others.
And they seem so happy about it!
Thank you, God, for people like that.

Let's pray for people . . .

We pray for people whose vision is limited,
who are so blinded by wealth and things
that they've lost sight of what really matters.
Please God, help all of us
– because we all do that sometimes –
to keep our values focused.

Gee whiz

Based on Luke 14:15-21

I don't know what gets into Mr Gee, sometimes. Mr Gee's my boss by the way – I'm his butler and personal servant. Now, where was I? Oh, yes – take the other week, for example. I knew he was planning a party, because it always gets him excited. 'Hey, Gabby,' he said. I do wish he wouldn't call me that – Gabriel's bad enough, but 'Gabby'! – but he's the boss, so how can I argue? 'Gabby,' he said, 'guess what I'm going to do.'

'From your tone of voice, sir, and from the way you have just addressed me, I surmise that you are planning a celebration.' I always talk like that to my boss – he thinks it sounds like a proper butler.

'You betcha sweet life, Gabby, baby – a party to end all parties.'

'And is there any specific reason for this event, sir?' I asked.

Mr Gee gave me his 'What sort of question is that?' look, and said, 'Does there need to be? Life, Gabby, life – that's what we're celebrating.'

I knew it was no good arguing when he was in that kind of mood, so I went and got his diary, found a free evening and got on my bike – Mr Gee likes his invitations delivered personally.

Hiram, the butcher, was really pleased. 'One of Mr Gee's parties!' he said. 'Of course, I'll be there. Just you try and stop me.'

Next, I went to see Martha – found her scrubbing the windows of her house. 'I just can't get this clean,' she said. 'Just one little bit of dirt that really won't come off. I've tried everything.'

A story, a hug and a prayer

'Cheap white wine,' I told her. 'That will move anything.* Now, Mr Gee's holding a party next Friday and would like to invite you.'

'Oh, how lovely,' Martha answered. 'I'll be there – I'd better wash my best frock and polish my bracelet.'

Barney the farmer seemed glad, too. 'I'll bring the cows home early that day,' he said, 'to make sure I get there on time.'

So, the great day came and Mr Gee was as high as a kite, as you'd expect. 'Everything ready, Gabby? Good, good, well, don't just stand there – go and get 'em – ooh, I can't wait for the party.'

Really – you'd have thought he was a child – sometimes Mr Gee can be so undignified! Anyway, I went round to Martha first. 'Party? What party?' she snapped. 'I haven't got time for parties – just taken over a new allotment – got to go and look at it – bet it'll be covered in weeds. Look, just tell Mr Gee I'm sorry, OK?'

Hiram was no better. 'Keep your voice down, Gabby,' he hissed, 'the wife will hear you. I got married the other day, and there's no way I can go out to a party. Give my apologies, will you?'

So I went to Barney. 'Gabriel!' he beamed. 'You're just in time to see my new cattle being delivered – really good beasts they are. What's that? Party? At a time like this? Sorry, tell Mr Gee some other time.'

Mr Gee was hopping mad. 'I'm going to have a party,' he shouted at me, 'even if the only guests I have are the local tramps. Now, there's an idea – they'd appreciate my kindness, wouldn't they! Off you go, Gabby, and get them in. The scruffier the better.'

I couldn't believe it. 'Sir,' I said, 'perhaps I should check that I correctly apprehend your meaning. You wish me to go into the street and bring in the persons of low social position, no financial means and unseemly appearance to attend your party?'

---

* Don't bank on it!

Gee whiz

'You got a problem with that?' The look in Mr Gee's eye said he wasn't to be trifled with, so I went. Of course, they came in by the dozen – no second invitation needed for them. Their table manners were terrible – they didn't even know which fork to use for their *hors d'ouvres* – and of course there are no washing facilities on the streets, where they live, so the smell was awful. But Mr Gee didn't mind – in fact he seemed to get more excited with each new arrival. 'Come and sit down,' he would say. 'Gabby, go and put some more food in the oven.'

The party seemed to go on for ever. Eventually, Mr Gee took pity on me and told me to go to bed. The last thing I remember is that they were dancing a conga from the dining table out into the fountain in the garden – and I mean, into, not round. And who do you think was leading it? Yes, you've got it. Sometimes I think I just don't understand Mr Gee, at all.

A story, a hug and a prayer

Let's chat . . .

He's always at it – God, that is.
He sends out invitations,
every moment of every day,
to every part of the universe.
'Come and share my love,' they say.

We're sad . . .

We want to say yes.
Honest, God, we do.
It's just that so many things get in the way
and we get sidetracked.
Can you help us to change, please?

We're glad . . .

And still you love us!
Thank you, God,
for not giving us up!

Let's pray for people . . .

Let's pray for people with good intentions,
but no time to turn them into reality.
Please, God, bless busy people,
and help them find time for you
– and each other
– and themselves.

Don't miss the party

Based on Luke 15:11-32

Jesus was in one of his story-telling moods. He'd just told a story about a woman who had 100 coins and lost one. She searched the whole house until she found it. Just before that, he'd also told almost exactly the same story, but about a shepherd who lost one of his 100 sheep and wouldn't give up searching until he'd saved it and brought it home. Then he went on to tell a story a little bit like this one.

There was once a rich farmer – we'll call him Tom – who had two sons. Two very different sons. One day, the younger one had something to say.

'Father,' he said, 'I have something to say.'

'Go on, Barney,' said his dad. (Did I tell you his name was Barney? Well, you know now, anyway.)

'Well,' Barney said, 'I know I'm going to get a share of your money when you die, but could I have it now? I mean, by the time you die I'll be old, like you are now, and I won't be able to enjoy it. Go on, Dad, please give it to me now.'

Tom wasn't happy about it. 'I'll bet he'll waste it,' he thought, 'but he's a big boy, now.' So Tom gave half his money to Barney, who jumped on a camel and disappeared in a cloud of dust.

Barney kept on going until he reached a country a long way away from home – a country full of exciting things – a country where you could dance all night, and where people were really, really friendly – as long as you had money. And Barney had money. A *lot* of money.

Not for long though. Not for long at all, at the rate he spent it. Very soon, what with the parties, the fancy clothes and a few more things best not mentioned here, Barney

A story, a hug and a prayer

spent all the money and had to get a job. Well, it was either that or go home to his father. And he couldn't go home – not with his elder brother, Jake, just waiting to sneer at him. Jake wouldn't have done anything stupid like this – Jake was a good boy, Jake was. Anyway, back to Barney. He got a job looking after pigs – the pay was nearly as bad as the smell, but beggars can't be choosers. Then he started thinking.

'Last week, I was having a party with 100 people who pretended they were my friends, and now I'm up to my knees in pigswill,' he thought. 'Mind you, there's not much difference in some ways – except that the pigs have better manners. This is ridiculous – my father's farm workers are better off than I am. Well, that's it. I'm going home. I'll ask Dad for a job. On second thoughts, I'll grovel. *Then* I'll ask Dad for a job.'

Back home at the farm, Tom was looking out for Barney – just as he had been every day – and saw him coming from a long way off. 'He's here!' he shouted. 'Barney's home!' and he went running out to meet him. He didn't listen to Barney's grovelling – just threw his arms round him and hugged him. 'Never mind the past,' he said. 'You're home, and that's all that matters.' Then he called out to a farm-hand, 'Hey, Zebedee, go kill something – preferably something we can eat – we're going to have a party!'

Tom found some beautiful new clothes for Barney, and sent him off to get washed and changed before the party. Well, he had to – the state Barney was in, no one would have wanted to dance with him. When the party began it was like nothing Barney had known before – much better than all the parties he'd had when he was busy wasting his dad's money. But there was one person who wasn't happy about it.

Barney's brother, Jake – remember Jake? – came in from working in the fields and asked what the party was about. When they told him he nearly hit the roof! 'I've been a really good prig to you – sorry, son to you!' he roared at his father. 'And do I get a party? Not rotten likely. But this son of yours wastes everything and you do this for him.'

Don't miss the party

'You're my son,' Tom answered. 'You don't want for any-thing. But your brother who we thought was lost is now found. He could have been dead – now he's alive. Can't you celebrate that? Come and join the party.'

I won't tell you what Jake answered, but I don't think his dad was very proud of it. So the story ended, with poor, good, deserving Jake shutting himself out of the party because he couldn't stand the idea that someone who *wasn't* good was getting a bit of love.

Funny things, people!

A story, a hug and a prayer

Let's chat . . .

It does seem unfair, doesn't it?
Someone who behaves like that
deserves to be punished – not given a party!
There again, I'm glad
God doesn't always give me what I deserve!

We're sad . . .

Is that how we are, Jesus?
Too hung up on 'justice' to appreciate love?
Please help us to be glad
when people turn back to you.

We're glad . . .

What an amazing way to love!
Are you like Barney's father, God?
Do you wait patiently
for us to come to our senses?
And then celebrate when we do?
Now, isn't that something!

Let's pray for people . . .

Some people are afraid to turn back to you, God.
They're afraid they'll be punished
– often because of what your 'friends' have told them!
Please give us all a better vision of your love,
and help everyone to feel they can turn to you.

Seth in a sweat

Based on Luke 16:19-31

This story is based on one that Jesus told – but I've changed it a little bit to give it a happy ending. I thought you might prefer that, and the point's still the same. It's all about a man we're going to call Seth. Seth lived in a big house, with big gardens, and very big gates to keep out poor people like Lazarus.

'Can't anyone get rid of that Lazarus guy?' Seth complained one day. 'He lies out there by the gate, all covered in sores – totally lowers the tone of the neighbourhood. Amos, you're my security guard – get him shifted.'

'Can't touch him, I'm afraid,' Amos replied. 'Not that I'd want to, anyway, but as long as he stays outside he's entitled to be there.'

'People like him aren't entitled to *be*, at all,' Seth complained. 'Just knowing he's there puts me off my dinner – talking of which, what's Cook preparing for tonight?'

'I believe, sir, that it's fresh avocados, followed by poached salmon in mushroom and tarragon sauce, with profiteroles and chocolate sauce for dessert.'

Seth pouted: 'Oh, it'll do, I suppose – but I expect something less ordinary for tomorrow.'

'Very well, sir. I'll pass the message on.'

'Yes, well, on your way to the kitchen go past the main gate and give that Lazarus a kick in the ribs – he might get the message and go away.'

Seth ate well that night. In fact, he ate much better than he slept – he should have remembered that tarragon gave him nightmares. It started with him feeling very hot and very uncomfortable. Then he realised he didn't recognise

A story, a hug and a prayer

his bedroom at all. He was surrounded by an eerie mist, and there was a smell of sulphur in the air. He strained his eyes to see through the mist, and as it began to clear he could see that he was looking through some big iron gates into a banqueting hall – and guess who was sitting at the table?

'Hey, what's that Lazarus doing in there?' he shouted. 'Who let him into my house?'

Then he realised, it wasn't his house – it just looked like it. Gradually, the truth dawned on him. 'I've died. I've died, and gone to – oh, no! No, it can't be!' Still sweating in the heat, he peered through the mist again, and saw Lazarus wasn't alone. His companion was a very old man, with a long beard and sharp, sparkling eyes.

'Hi, there, Seth! You know me – Abraham's the name! Sorry about the heating, but that's how it's always been where you are. Now, this – well, this is heaven! But you know how good this is, don't you – you had it all your life, so we thought it was Lazarus' turn, now.'

'Well, can you just ask him to bring me a drink of water?' Seth begged. 'It's horrible out here.'

Abraham looked sad. 'Can't be done, old lad,' he answered. 'Pity, but there it is. It's those gates, you see – no one seems to be able to find the key. A bit like when you were alive, isn't it – except, the other way round, of course. Oh, well, that's death, I suppose.'

Seth knew it was no good arguing. 'OK, so no one can help me now,' he said. 'But what about my brothers – they're still alive on earth, and if Lazarus could just pop back there and warn them, perhaps they'll have a chance to be nicer people so they don't end up like me.'

'What's up?' Abraham demanded. 'All that expensive education and they can't read? It's all in their Bibles if they care to look.'

'Oh, Bibles, Bibles,' Seth said, impatiently. 'You know no one reads them – but if someone went back from the dead . . .'

Abraham interrupted. 'If they don't listen to the prophets, why should they listen to someone who comes back from

Seth in a sweat

the dead?' He turned away. 'More wine, Lazarus? It's a very good year.'

Suddenly, Seth stopped sweating and felt very cold. A howling wind seemed to be cutting right through his body. Abraham and Lazarus had disappeared, and there was nothing but blackness – and that terrible draught. Seth gradually came to, back in his own bedroom with the bed-clothes all crumpled up on the floor. 'What a nightmare,' he thought. 'I never want to experience that again. Locked out, watching someone else enjoy all the good things of life – how absolutely awful!'

Then he thought for a minute. 'Amos!' he bellowed. 'Go and open the gate and get that poor Lazarus in – things are going to change around here.'

A story, a hug and a prayer

Let's chat . . .

Do we ever find poor people an inconvenience?
Do we ever wish they'd go away?
Perhaps one day they will
– when they're no longer poor . . .

We're sad . . .

Sorry, God!
Not that we've got enough to eat
– we're not sorry about that!
We're sorry that sometimes
we tend to blame other people
as if poverty were their fault.
Please help us to be more caring.

We're glad . . .

Thank you, God, for every kind person.
Thank you for people who've helped us
when we've been in any kind of trouble.
Thank you for the love you've put into the world.

Let's pray for people . . .

Some people seem to spend all their time
on the outskirts of life*
Please help us all to notice,
and find ways of including them.

---

* You might like to flip through the Gospels sometime and see how often Jesus meets people at the edge of the town. Very symbolic!

Healing of 10 lepers

Based on Luke 17:11-19

This is a story about some very fed-up people.

'I'm fed up!' said Nick.

'Me, too – I'm fed up, as well,' added Ben.

'I bet you're not as fed up as I am!' Jake chimed in.

Now, this was in danger of getting silly – especially since there were 10 of them in the group. So it's a good thing Nick spoke next or it could be a very boring dialogue. 'What I'm really fed up with,' he said, 'is not having anywhere to call home. The people in Galilee don't want us, so we move to Samaria, but they don't want us either. I mean, what *are* we supposed to do?'

'Not have a skin disease, I suppose,' Jake answered.

Ben snapped back: 'Oh, that's really helpful, isn't it – did you think of that all by yourself? Does stating the blindingly obvious come naturally to you, or did you go to college to learn it? The point is we *have* got a skin disease. I mean, be honest, would *you* want to stand next to yourself in the queue at the bakery?'

'It's not fair, though,' Jake butted in. 'We didn't ask for this, and it doesn't change the kind of people we are – so we get left out of everything just because other people can't hack a bit of flaky skin!'

It's probably a good thing that something happened to take their minds off it, because they'd had this conversation lots of times, and it didn't change anything – just made them all the angrier. What happened was a group of people coming along the road toward them.

'Oh-oh!' said Jake. 'Time to take cover, before they start throwing things at us.'

A story, a hug and a prayer

'Oh, yes, of course!' Ben responded, angrily. 'This really is the life, isn't it – ducking and diving every time we see someone else: "Sorry for being ill, your honour" . . . "Please forgive me for breathing, your healthiness" . . . "Excuse me while I just crawl out of your way, reverend sir"! Well, that's it! I'm not running and hiding from anyone any more. I'm staying here!'

Nick was staring very hard at the other group. 'Just a minute,' he said. 'I know that crowd – it's Jesus and his friends. They're still far enough away not to be frightened of us, so let's give Jesus a shout.' Then, without waiting for them to agree, he started yelling out, 'Hey! Jesus! Sir! Can you do us a favour?'

Jesus came closer so that he could see what was the matter. 'Go and let the priests take a look at you,' he said, 'and you'll be fine.' That was because the priests in those days had the job of infection control. If they said you were infectious, you were infectious – and if they said you weren't then people would talk to you again! So the 10 people took off to find the nearest priest, and as they were going their skin healed up and was all soft and smooth like new.

Nick stopped in his tracks. 'Got to go and thank Jesus,' he said.

Jake couldn't believe his ears. 'What?' he said, 'waste time on silly social conventions like saying thank you? Don't be daft – come on and see the priest.'

Nick was determined, though. 'Even if you won't,' he said, 'I will.' So the other nine carried on looking for a priest and Nick turned round to go back to where he'd met Jesus. When he got there, he just threw himself down on the ground in front of Jesus and kept on saying: 'Thank you, Jesus! Thank you so much!'

Now, the interesting thing I haven't told you, is that Nick was a Samaritan – and Samaritans and Jews didn't normally have a good word to say for each other. So Jesus was a bit surprised. 'I thought there were 10 people that I healed,' he mused. 'And out of all that, can it really be that

Healing of 10 lepers

only one had the decency to come back and praise God for it – and him a foreigner, too!' Then he turned to Nick. 'Up you get, and on you go,' he said. 'Your faith's made you well.'

A story, a hug and a prayer

Let's chat . . .

Saying 'Thank you' really isn't difficult,
is it?
In fact, sometimes it's too easy.
This guy had to break off an important journey,
at the height of his excitement,
and run all the way back.
Now, that's *appreciation!*

We're sad . . .

We often don't appreciate
the things you give us.
Please, God, help us to be more appreciative
of your love and goodness.

We're glad . . .

Now we actually stop to think of it,
you really do give us an awful lot, don't you!*
Thank you, God!

Let's pray for people . . .

Some people are always taken for granted
– never seem to be valued.
Please God, help us and others
to find ways of showing them
a bit of appreciation.

---

* Can you think of some examples?

140

Danny sees the light

Based on Luke 18:9-14

Jesus was getting well fed up. He'd just about had it with people who went strutting around the place thinking they were better than everybody else and making other people feel bad. So he told a story a little like this one.

Danny is a really unhappy man. Oh, he's done well enough in life – or so a lot of people would think: he's got the house, the car, the clothes, all the lifestyle of a guy who's doing well. The only thing he hasn't got is friends – because the way he's got all the other things has made him very unpopular. He's the kind of guy who never misses a chance to take advantage of someone. Honesty, he believes, is only the best policy in story books – in real life you have to grab what you can. So he's grabbed and grabbed all his life – and now, the only things he hasn't got are things money can't buy.

Well, on this particular day, he's walking past a church, and he decides to go in. For some reason, he feels scared – as if he shouldn't be there – so he just creeps in and stands for a while at the back, thinking about how there must be more to life than grabbing what you can while you're here. 'It's ridiculous!' he's thinking. 'I'm nearly 60 years old, and I might as well be dead for all it matters! No one would miss me if I were!' Gradually, the silence and the peace of the place begin to get to him, and he realises he's never had any peace in his life. 'This is the first time,' he thinks, 'that I've ever just stood and stared when I could have been go-getting. And the silly thing is, I like it!'

Suddenly, he gets a great sense of waste. 'What've I done with my life?' he asks himself, and immediately answers,

A story, a hug and a prayer

'Frittered it away, that's what.' Eventually, he can't hold back any longer. 'God forgive me!' he shouts. 'God forgive me for wasting his gift of life – and for spoiling other people's!'

His voice echoes round the huge empty building – except that it isn't empty. Danny's horrified to hear another, softer voice: 'My word, that came from the heart, didn't it!'

Before he has time to curl up with shame, Danny finds himself staring into a pair of twinkling eyes and a big, friendly smile. 'Hi,' the smile says. 'I'm Juliet – it's my turn on the cleaning rota. Sorry, did you want to be on your own for a bit?'

'On my own? Do I want to be on my own?' It's as if the woman's seen right into his soul – and got it completely wrong! 'I've been on my own all my life,' he hears himself saying, 'and it's the last place I want to be.' Then he collects his thoughts. 'I'm sorry about just now – how embarrassing!'

'Sorry?' Juliet echoes. 'Why sorry? Look, I come here every Sunday – and some weekdays, like now – and I've heard prayers but never one as good as yours. There's one of our regulars – comes here most weeks – spends all his time thanking God for making him such a good person. Always going on, he is – giving his "testimony" he calls it. Bragging, *I* call it. "Oh, thank you, God," he'll say – "thank you for making me so good. Since I found you I've never put a foot wrong – I keep all the rules, give just the right amount of my money to charity, come to worship regularly . . ." '

Juliet snorted. 'I tell, you, he's not praying to God – he's talking to himself. Probably doesn't really know the difference, if you ask me. If you could hear some of the God-bothering that passes for religion in this place, you'd be proud of what you just said.'

Danny's really gobsmacked by this. He's never been proud of anything in his life – not really, truly, deep-down proud. It's as if he's been set free – free to be himself and not someone else.

Suddenly, he's on his feet. 'Thank you!' he's saying, over

Danny sees the light

and over again as he shakes Juliet's hand. 'You've really helped me – but now I've got to go. I've got a lot of thinking to do and changes to make.'

He turns and walks along the aisle until he's almost at the door, before he stops for a moment and turns round to where Juliet's watching him. 'You know, I've never bothered with all that God stuff,' he says, 'but if God's anything like you, he's OK.'

A story, a hug and a prayer

Let's chat . . .

> *Just get a load of that other guy*
> *– the one Juliet talked about!*
> *Holier-than-thou doesn't begin to describe it!*
> *Religion isn't about doing things for God*
> *– it's about being on his wavelength!*

We're sad . . .

> *We all do it, sometimes, God:*
> *get so hung up on doing the religious stuff*
> *that we forget just to listen to you.*
> *Help us to take time*
> *to hear what you're trying to say to us.*

We're glad . . .

> *Thank you, God, for those special moments*
> *when you really cut through all the nonsense*
> *and help us to see things differently.*
> *Would that happen more often, perhaps,*
> *if we cut the cackle and gave you a bit of space?*

Let's pray for people . . .

> *It's sad, Lord.*
> *Some people spend all their time*
> *trying to please you by doing religious things,*
> *when what you most want us to do*
> *is be good to ourselves and each other.*
> *Please help us all to know you better.*

He's the greatest!

Based on Luke 22:7-27

It was Passover time – the greatest festival of the Jewish year – and the big question all Jesus' disciples were asking was, 'Where are we going to celebrate it?' Now, most people would celebrate it at home – but Jesus and his friends hadn't got one.

'It's all arranged,' Jesus answered. 'Peter, James and John are going to go and get the room ready. Just go into the city and look out for a man carrying a big jar of water, and follow where he leads.'

Peter scoffed out loud. 'A *man*, carrying water? That's women's work!'

James added, 'Look, Jesus, I don't mind following you, even if you are a bit out of the ordinary, but I'm not following any guy who hasn't got it in him to make his wife do the housework.'

'Too right,' John agreed. 'We've got some pride, you know.'

'Yes, I do know,' Jesus answered. 'And that's the first thing you're going to have to change. Look, just do it, OK?'

'OK, OK,' Peter said. 'At least he'll be easy to find – I mean how many blokes would be seen in public carrying a water jug?'

'Exactly,' said Jesus. 'He'll take you to the house, and there'll be a room all set out ready for us. You've just got the food to sort out.'

So, that evening, Jesus sat down for supper with his closest friends. 'I've *so* been looking forward to this,' he said. 'Things are going to get rough, and I really wanted to share this Passover meal with you first – because it's the last one I'll eat before God's kingdom comes.'

A story, a hug and a prayer

Then he took a loaf of bread. He said the blessing, broke it apart and gave it to them to share. 'Think of this as my body,' he said. 'It's given for you. Do this, in remembrance of me.'

James was puzzled. '"In remembrance"? Is he going to snuff it or something?'

'Don't be daft!' Peter retorted. 'He can't do that – God's got big plans for him.'

'Oh, we know,' John cut in. 'And we're part of them, James and I – we're going to be real big shots – we've already put a word in.'

I won't bore you with the rest of the conversation – very childish, it was. After the supper, Jesus took a large cup of wine. Again he said a blessing, and then passed it round for them to share. 'See this cup?' he said. 'Wine, poured out for the good of you all – just like my blood will be.'

John shuddered – didn't like that image at all – but Jesus just went on talking.

'It'll mean a whole new way of life – a new relationship with God.'

Well, no one quite understood what Jesus was saying. They just got the idea that things were going to be different, and Jesus was going to have to go through a horrible ordeal to bring it about.

'It's the revolution!' Peter exclaimed. 'It's all going to happen tonight – don't you see? Now, don't worry – when Jesus makes me the boss, I'll see you're all taken care of.'

'You – the boss?' James answered. 'I'll tell you what you'll be: you'll be a nothing, that's what – all mouth and no action, that's you. Now, when it comes to being top dog in the new world, there's only one choice, and you're looking at him.'

'Oh, do shut up, you two,' John butted in, 'or I'll put you both out to grass – because the big noise around here's going to be me.'

Before long, all the other disciples had joined in and there was a real old ding-dong going on around the table – and Jesus was really fed up.

He's the greatest!

'Haven't you lot learned anything, after all this time?' he said, when he'd managed to quieten them. 'That's all old-world stuff – it's how people outside God's kingdom live, not inside it. Kings put on airs and graces – and everybody thinks the bosses are doing them a great favour by shoving them around. Not for you though – oh, no! Any one of you who wants to be really great is going to have to be like the baby of the family. You want to be leader? Be a servant.'

By now, they were all staring at him, open-mouthed. 'Well, look at me,' Jesus went on. 'Look at what's happening here. Who's greatest, the one who sits and eats food, or the waiter who serves it? Isn't it the one who gets waited on who's the greatest? But here am I, waiting on you. You want greatness? You'd better learn to follow my example – and not sneering at men who carry water would be a start!'

It took an awfully long time for Jesus' friends to learn that lesson – and most of us are still struggling with it!

A story, a hug and a prayer

Let's chat . . .

*Now, don't tell me you've never taken
a bit of secret pleasure
in doing better than someone else;
I know I have.
It's not unnatural –
just doesn't really help anybody!*

We're sad . . .

*We've all done it, Jesus:
wanted to be the 'top dog',
maybe even been secretly a little pleased
about someone else's failure.
We're not proud of it.
Not proud of it at all.
Please help us to do it less.*

We're glad . . .

*Even when we get it wrong, though,
you love us
just as you loved those disciples!
Thank you, Jesus!*

Let's pray for people . . .

*We pray for people
who think coming second is failure.
We also pray for those of us
who can never even get anywhere near second!
Please help us all to find our true greatness
in caring for one another.*

He's alive!

Based on Luke 23:44-24:11

Jesus' enemies thought they'd won, when they saw him nailed to the cross and killed, but they couldn't have been more wrong. Even there, Jesus showed that love can be stronger than hatred. He never cursed anyone – he even prayed for the people who were torturing him – and he comforted the criminal who was dying on the cross next to him. And the last words he said were words of faith. 'Father,' he said, 'I commend my soul into your care.'

Standing at the foot of the cross was a tough soldier – a hard man, who'd seen a lot of death – and even he couldn't help being impressed. 'What a man!' he said. 'He truly was a completely good man!'

Standing further away were some of the women who were friends of Jesus. They'd never left him, even at the most dangerous moments, but had stayed there to show they cared. 'You ought to go home,' said a passing man. 'This is no place for women.'

Joanna answered, 'Well, someone's got to be here to share his last moments with him – we're not going to let him die alone.' Then, when they knew it was all over, she turned to Mary Magdalene and said, 'Let's go and see where they bury Jesus – then we can come back later to pay our respects.'

Stealthily, not wanting to attract attention, they followed the men who were burying Jesus. They saw him placed hurriedly in a hole in the hillside, with a big stone rolled in front to seal it. 'After the religious festival's over,' said Mary, 'we'll come back and make sure he's given a *decent* burial.'

So it was that, early on the Sunday morning, the same women – Joanna, Mary Magdalene and the other Mary who

A story, a hug and a prayer

was James' mother – all met with jars of spice and perfume to go to Jesus' grave. 'How are we going to move that big stone away from the grave?' asked Mary Magdalene.

'I don't know,' said the other Mary. 'Let's worry about that when we get there.'

'A lot of people would say we're mad, anyway,' Joanna commented, 'but these things matter. Jesus always cared about other people, so now we're going to do the right thing by him.'

They walked silently in the early dawn light until they came within sight of the tomb, and they stopped in amazement and horror. 'Someone's opened it already,' gasped Joanna. 'The stone's been rolled away.'

'Someone's up to no good,' Mary Magdalene murmured quietly. 'Can't they just let him rest in peace?'

Slowly, they moved nearer to the tomb and peered in. It looked very spooky, but as their eyes got used to the low light they saw something that made them stop in amazement.

Nothing.

Jesus' body wasn't there.

They were staring open-mouthed at one another when suddenly the place was filled with light, and two men in dazzling white clothes stood in front of them. 'Why are you looking in a grave for someone who's alive?' one of them asked. 'Jesus isn't here – he's risen from the dead!' The women were terrified, but gradually the truth sank in as the man continued talking. 'Remember what he told you while he was with you before – how he'd be killed by his enemies but would rise again on the third day? Well, this is it!'

Suddenly, everything fell into place. Of course – God had raised Jesus to new life, just as Jesus had said that he would. The women didn't know whether to laugh or cry for joy!

'Fancy us being the first to know,' exclaimed Mary Magdalene.

'Not so surprising,' Joanna replied. 'After all, we stayed with him – and we're here now.'

'Come on!' cried the other Mary. 'We've got to tell the others.'

He's alive!

What a sight they were – stumbling over tree roots, tripping over the hems of their skirts, and laughing joyfully all the time, as they ran to where they knew the disciples were hiding. 'He's alive! He's alive! Really, he is – just as he promised he would be!'

At first, none of the men believed them – they thought they'd been dreaming or something. But soon the whole world was going to be buzzing with the good news: Jesus is alive!

A story, a hug and a prayer

Let's chat . . .

> *Those women were probably the only ones*
> *who didn't leave Jesus*
> *when the going got tough.*
> *And they were the first ones*
> *to know about the resurrection!*

We're sad . . .

> *There have been times, Jesus,*
> *when people have needed us*
> *and we've left them to cope.*
> *Perhaps we were afraid,*
> *or we just couldn't watch.*
> *Maybe we preferred to pretend*
> *that it wasn't happening.*
> *Please forgive us.*

We're glad . . .

> *Thank you for being there, Jesus,*
> *when things are bad for us*
> *– even when we don't realise you were there*
> *until we look back.*
> *Thank you for all the times*
> *that you bring new life out of bad times.*

Let's pray for people . . .

> *Sometimes it just seems that there's no hope.*
> *Thank you God, for being there,*
> *and for the people – like these women –*
> *who make you easier to see*
> *by being there themselves.*
> *Please encourage and strengthen them.*

Chateau heaven, '27

Based on John 2:1-11

Can you imagine having a party and running out of food, because your parents hadn't provided enough? I mean, would that be embarrassing, or would that be embarrassing? Well, that's probably how Tom and Becky felt at their wedding, when the wine ran out.

'Someone didn't order enough of it,' Tom said angrily.

'Oh, that's right,' Becky answered, 'find someone to blame, just as long as it isn't you.'

'Now, now, you two,' came a friendly voice, 'try not to have a row at your own wedding – you've got a whole lifetime for that sort of thing. Let's see what can be done about it before everybody notices and it all gets ugly.'

The voice belonged to Mary, and she turned to her son who was there with some of his friends – right in the middle of an interesting conversation.

'Oh, come off it, Jesus,' Simon was saying, 'if Sumarcus hadn't made an unscheduled pit stop, he'd have won that chariot race by a lap.'

'Right, Jesus, my lad,' Mary interrupted, briskly, 'time to make yourself useful – they've run out of wine.'

'Oh, really, Mother!' Jesus answered. 'Since when were you and I in the catering business? Look, I don't want to get into all that stuff yet – it's not time.'

Mary gave her son an old-fashioned look – before she turned to a couple of waiters standing nearby, and said, 'Just do whatever he tells you – OK? He's a good boy, underneath it all – he won't let you down.'

Now, standing near the door were some big water tubs. And I mean big – around, oh, 20 gallons, maybe 30, in each.

A story, a hug and a prayer

They were used for washing guests' feet when they arrived, and yes, I know it's a rather strange way of saying, 'How nice of you to come,' but when everyone wears open sandals and the roads are made of pure dust, well, it's the polite thing to do – or at least, it was then. Jesus looked across at the water containers and said, 'Oh, I think they'll do.'

Tom wasn't exactly happy, and Becky was rapidly losing what was left of her cool. 'You give that to my guests to drink,' she said, 'and I'll never speak to you again.' Then she turned to Tom, 'But *you* won't get off so lightly – I'll have a few things to say to you.'

Oh, dear! Now, you or I might have been a bit fazed by that – but not Jesus. 'Top up the jars,' he told the waiters, 'fill them right to the brim.'

The waiters looked at one another in disbelief, but they did as they were told – arguing with Jesus would have been one thing, but his mother was quite another proposition. 'Now, pour some of it out and take it to the caterer to taste,' Jesus said.

The waiters' hands were shaking as they lifted the heavy jars between them and began to pour the water into a jug. But, hang on a minute – what was happening? The water was a very funny colour. Nothing strange in that, of course – people weren't that fussy what kind of water they used for washing guests' feet – but this water wasn't dirty; it was a rich, deep red. The waiters were amazed, and went to take some to the caterer to taste.

'Well done, Jesus,' Mary beamed, 'I knew you wouldn't let me down.'

Becky still wasn't happy, though. 'Look,' she said, 'anyone can play tricks with a bit of food colouring – you just wait until the caterer tastes it. Oh, it's going to be *so* embarrassing!'

They turned to see the waiter pouring some of the liquid into a cup for the caterer to try. 'Any moment, now . . .' said Becky to Tom. 'If you've embarrassed me in front of all our friends, I'll never speak to you again – you're pathetic!'

The caterer took a sip of the wine, and his face broke into a big smile of approval before he finished off the cup,

Chateau heaven, '27

and the waiters started serving it to the guests. One of them went over to Tom. 'He's well pleased,' he told him. 'Most weddings we do, they use the best wine first – then when everyone's too plastered to notice they serve up the rubbish. He reckons you've saved the best of the wine until the end.'

Becky squealed with delight, and threw her arms around Tom's neck. 'Darling!' she gushed. 'I never doubted you for a minute!'

Mary gave Jesus a proud smile that seemed to say, 'That's my lovely boy,' but fortunately Jesus didn't notice. He was back to his conversation with Simon.

'I'll say this for you, Jesus,' Simon said. 'You may not have a clue about chariot racing, but you certainly know your wine.'

A story, a hug and a prayer

Let's chat . . .

Sometimes, we religious people
can be so stuffy, can't we!
You'd hardly think God intended life to be celebrated
– like a wedding!

We're sad . . .

How is it, God,
that some people have the idea
that religion's all about not enjoying life?
Who's given them that kind of idea, we wonder?
Please forgive us if we've ever forgotten
that life is your gift, to be celebrated.

We're glad . . .

Thank you, God, for all the people we know
who make life good for us.
Thank you for all those
who show us your love
and help us to celebrate it.

Let's pray for people . . .

Far too many people have been taught
to feel guilty about being happy!
Please help all people to know your love,
and that you want them to have
the best possible life!

Help me feed the world

Based on John 6:1-14

I tell you, it was the most amazing thing of my life. I remember, I was about 10 years old at the time, and everybody made me feel it. Young, that is. If it wasn't, 'You're too young to understand,' it was, 'Go and play while your mother and I talk about something important.' Not that I had bad parents mind you – that's how it was for kids in those days.

My mum explained it all to me. 'One day, Ben,' she said – that's my name, Ben – 'One day, Ben, you'll be grown up, and you'll be important. But now – well, go and play somewhere, there's a good boy.' Sometimes, it made me hopping mad – I mean, I may be a kid but I'm not stupid. You know, I look around at the world the way the grown-ups have made it, and – well, if that's how clever they are I'm not impressed. I mean, I'm *seriously* not impressed.

Then Jesus came to town – well, to the hills outside it, but that's near enough. Everyone was going to see him – everyone except my mum and dad, who had something important to do, as usual. 'You can go, if you like,' Mum said. 'I'll pack you up a bit of lunch, and while you're away your dad and I can decide what colour to paint your bedroom. Yes, I know you want yellow walls, but we'll decide what's right for you.'

So that's how I came to be out in the hills, with a full lunch pack and an empty schedule, just waiting to see what Jesus would say. And a good thing too – if I hadn't been there, I don't know what would have happened. The place was absolutely crowded, and there seemed to be some kind of argument going on among Jesus' friends.

A story, a hug and a prayer

'Don't blame me, it's not my fault,' I heard Philip saying.

'I'm not blaming you, Phil,' Jesus answered. 'I'm just asking, that's all – where can we get some food for all these people?'

Well, I knew I hadn't got much, but it would be a start, so I went up to one of the gang and said, 'You can have my lunch if you'd like it.'

He smiled very kindly – you know, the way grown-ups do when they're trying to humour you – and said: 'It's nice of you, sonny.' (Don't you just hate being called names like that?) 'It's nice of you, sonny, but you leave this to us.'

Well, I'd had enough of that kind of thing from my parents, without getting it from complete strangers, too. I know it wasn't very polite, but I couldn't help saying: 'You got a better idea?'

'Look here, kid,' Philip interrupted, 'I know you mean well, but this is grown-ups' stuff, OK?'

'Please yourself,' I said, and was about to go away when Andrew came over. I'd met Andrew before, and he's not bad as grown-ups go.

'What've you got?' he asked. And he didn't sneer when he saw it. 'Hey, Jesus,' he called, 'there's a lad here with five bread rolls and a couple of fish – not much for all these people, but how about it?'

I couldn't believe it – Jesus seemed really glad I was there. 'Hey, you guys,' he called to his friends, 'take a look at this. Is this terrific, or is this terrific? Well, don't just stand there – tell everyone to sit down, and then start serving.'

I don't know how Jesus did it, but everyone got fed – and I got plenty myself, as well. And afterwards, when we'd all eaten, he told us to collect up the bits people had dropped, so they wouldn't go to waste. Twelve baskets, we filled – no kidding, 12 – so there was more left over when he'd finished than I'd given him in the beginning. Weird – I mean, really weird.

When I got home, I couldn't wait to tell my mum and dad. 'Hey, guess what?' I said. 'I just helped Jesus feed 5000 people.'

Help me feed the world

'That's nice, dear,' said Mum. 'I hope you didn't get in the way. Now go and tidy your room while I get some dinner.'

Grown-ups – I ask you! Tell you one thing, I bet Jesus wouldn't send me away when I'd got something interesting to tell him.

A story, a hug and a prayer

Let's chat . . .

*It's easy just to take one look at people
and decide they haven't got anything to offer.
Maybe they don't look the part;
perhaps they're too young
or too old.
Sometimes, they surprise us,
thank God!*

We're sad . . .

*We're sorry, God,
for making snap judgements about people
because of their age, or their colour,
their gender or the way they're dressed.
Help us to be open-minded,
and give you a chance to work through them.*

We're glad . . .

*Thank you, God, for surprising us.
Thank you for old people with fresh, vibrant minds.
Thank you for children with so much to teach us.
Thank you for oddly dressed people
who are full of love.
Thank you for the unexpected!*

Let's pray for people . . .

*You know, God,
there are lots of people like that boy;
people who could change the world for us
if only we'd give them a chance.
Help us to appreciate them more.*

Sore feet and toffee noses

Based on John 13:3-17

Can you imagine a world where there are no cars or buses, so you have to walk everywhere? And it gets worse: trainers haven't been invented, and everyone just wears open sandals – and there are no proper roads or footpaths, so you get dust and mud all over your feet, and the grit gets between your toes and makes them sore.

Well, that's the world Jesus and his friends lived in. So they had a custom that people always kept clean water ready for guests to use – and if they had servants it was they who got the job of washing guests' feet. Everyone knew it was a horrible job, so most people were too proud to do it if they didn't have to. 'I wouldn't be seen dead, washing someone's feet,' they used to say – which of course they wouldn't. Who would? It would make a great headline, though, wouldn't it – 'Ghost Opens Foot-washing Salon' – I don't think so. Anyway, I digress – the point is it wasn't a job that someone with a social position to uphold would do.

Jesus did, though. He was having his last meal with his disciples, and he knew they still hadn't really learned his way of thinking. So he got up from the table, stripped to the waist and went and fetched a bowl of water and a towel.

'Hey,' Andrew said. 'What's going on? Why's the boss doing this job?'

'I don't know,' James answered. 'No sense of his own dignity, that's Jesus' trouble.'

Jesus ignored them and carried on – kneeling at their feet and bending over them as he lovingly removed every bit of mud and grit, and dried their feet with his towel.

Peter was getting more and more anxious. 'I can't have

A story, a hug and a prayer

this,' he thought. 'I have to look up to Jesus – if I can't look up to him, what does that make me?' And as he watched Jesus kneeling there, shuffling from feet to feet on his knees, he began to feel more and more embarrassed. When Jesus got to him, he couldn't contain himself.

'Hey, Jesus – no!' he said. 'You are not the slave around here. You are the Boss – the Big Cheese – He Who Must Be Obeyed. You do *not* wash feet. And you most definitely do not wash *my* feet.'

Jesus looked up at him. 'OK, if that's how you want it,' he said. 'But if you won't let me do this, then it's obvious you want me to be something I can't be – so I don't see how you can have any part in what I'm doing, really. Still, it's your decision.'

Well, Peter *thought* he was the strong one – solid as a rock, you might say – but in fact he could change faster than a politician with a bad poll rating when it suited him. 'Oh, well, why didn't you say so!' he said. 'In that case, you'd better not stop at my feet. There's my hands, my head – why not tip the bowl over me while you're at it?'

Jesus looked patient. 'No need to get carried away, Peter,' he said gently. 'Just your feet will do,' and he bent down to wash and dry Peter's feet. Then he got up, put his shirt back on and sat down again.

'D'you know what I've just done?' he asked. 'You call me the Boss, right? The Big Cheese – the Top Dog. I don't mind if you make me sound like something from a fast-food outlet, but you need to understand this: if I, whom you think of as the big-shot around here, have just washed your feet, then perhaps you shouldn't be too proud to do it for one another – unless of course you think you're greater than I am. This is what it's about in our community – we serve each other, and no one's too proud to do anything. Do you understand?'

'Sure do,' answered James. 'Does that mean it's your turn to wash up?'

Sore feet and toffee noses

Let's chat . . .

I don't know about you,
but I think doing great things is sometimes easier
than doing simple ones!
We can all make the big gestures occasionally:
buy a beautiful present, or throw a big party.
Jesus just washed his friends' feet!

We're sad . . .

Please forgive us, God,
for getting such big ideas that we neglect
the important things.
Help us to remember the value
of simple kindness.

We're glad . . .

We're grateful for people
who do the little things for us.
who remind us when we forget,
or who make sure there's toothpaste in the bathroom.
Thank you, God,
for people who care.

Let's pray for people . . .

Please God, bless all people
who do little things for others.
Let them know they're appreciated.
Oh, and while you're at it,
can you inspire some other people
to do little things for them?

Forgiveness that hurts

Based on John 21:9-23

Peter was feeling awkward. Only a few days ago, he'd been too frightened to admit he even knew Jesus – a real letdown, he'd turned out to be. Jesus' enemies were trying to kill him and they'd recognised Peter as one of Jesus' friends. Peter had done what – if we're honest – many of us might do. 'What, me?' he'd said. 'I don't know the guy from Adam – whoever *he* might have been.'

But they wouldn't stop – just went on and on accusing Peter of being one of Jesus' friends. Three times he'd said he wasn't, before he was overcome by guilt and ran off. So they put Jesus to death, and Peter felt absolutely terrible.

Now, of course, it was much later. Jesus had risen from the dead, and his friends were all wonderfully happy – but Peter felt embarrassed every time they met. And now, Jesus was cooking them all breakfast – being really kind to them – almost as though nothing had happened.

As they were eating, Jesus seemed to sense that Peter was feeling awkward. 'Simon,' he said. 'Simon, son of John, do you love me?'

Peter was startled. Jesus hadn't called him Simon for ages. He'd renamed him Peter, which meant 'rock', but now for some reason he'd gone back to Simon. 'Well,' Peter thought, 'I've hardly been a rock over the last few days, so perhaps I deserve it.' Then he said, 'Yes, Jesus, you know I love you – like my own brother, and then some.'

'Then you'll feed my lambs,' said Jesus. 'Won't you?'

Peter knew Jesus well enough to recognise the code: take care of my friends. Well, that was OK – it was the least he could do.

A story, a hug and a prayer

Then Jesus spoke again. 'Simon, son of John, d'you love me?'

'Of course I do, Jesus – you know that.'

'Then, take care of my sheep.'

The silence was heavy. Peter knew something was going on, but couldn't quite put his finger on it. Then Jesus spoke a third time. 'Simon, son of John, do you love me?'

Really, this was too much! 'That's three times he's asked that!' Peter thought, angrily, and he burst out, 'Look Jesus, you know perfectly well that I love you – after all, you know everything.'

Then he realised. Indeed, Jesus *did* know everything! He knew that Peter had pretended not to know him when he was in trouble. Three times Peter had denied being his friend. So now that Jesus was risen from the dead, he was giving Peter three chances to say that he *was*. Trust Jesus to do it this way – make him face up to what he'd done, and give him the chance to put it right. Most people would either have held a grudge or just pretended it was all OK, but Jesus knew better. Then Peter realised Jesus was speaking again.

'Feed my sheep,' Jesus said. 'You're going to need to be strong, Peter. It was OK when you were young, and you'd fasten up your belt and go wherever you wanted. One day you'll be old – and someone else will take you where you don't want to go at all. Know what I mean?'

Peter understood: one day, his faith would really be tested, and Jesus didn't want him letting himself down again.

'That's for later,' Jesus smiled. 'What you have to do for now is stick with me. OK?'

Peter's faith grew and he became one of the greatest Christians – not because he always got things right, but because he knew what it was to get things wrong. And most importantly he knew what it was to be forgiven.

Forgiveness that hurts

Let's chat . . .

Haven't we all had that guilty feeling,
and wished we could get it out in the open?
That's what Jesus did for Peter:
got it out in the open,
helped him face it
and cleared the air.
Now, that's friendship!

We're sad . . .

We're sorry, Jesus,
for the times we put off difficult conversations;
the times we've just let bad feelings fester,
because we haven't the courage to deal with them.
Please help us to be the kind of friends to others
that you are to us.

We're glad . . .

It's not always nice, is it, God,
when people make us face up to things.
True friends sometimes do that, though,
and it feels better afterwards.
Thank you, God, for real friends.

Let's pray for people . . .

Right now, in lots of places,
there are people who are feeling guilty,
or hurt, or frightened,
and are afraid to say so.
Please, God, find them a friend to help.